THE WHIGS OF FLORIDA
1845-1854
by *Herbert J. Doherty, Jr.*

University of Florida Monographs
SOCIAL SCIENCES
No. 1, Winter 1959

UNIVERSITY OF FLORIDA PRESS / GAINESVILLE, FLORIDA

EDITORIAL COMMITTEE

Social Sciences Monographs

FOREWORD

In keeping with its desire to encourage research in all branches of knowledge in which advanced degrees are awarded at the University of Florida, the Graduate School is establishing two monograph series, one in the humanities and one in the social sciences. With this purpose the administration of the University of Florida is in hearty accord, and I wish for these publications the kind of success that can result only from excellence.

There is general recognition throughout the nation that the humanities and social sciences have not been receiving the attention for their researches that has been given to the physical and biological sciences and the more applied areas of learning. In establishing these new publication channels the University is providing an added incentive for liberal scholarship and research.

Perhaps it is inevitable in the present state of world affairs that the balance of support will be weighted on the side of those studies which have as their aim the physical well-being of our people. However, I am keenly aware that if we are to maintain our civilization as well as our existence, energy must also be invested in those studies which have as their ultimate aim the understanding and cultivation of man's social and spiritual life. It is therefore a genuine pleasure to wish the Graduate School and the humanistic and social science faculties of the University great success in their work of scholarship and its dissemination.

J. WAYNE REITZ
PRESIDENT

A NOTE OF THANKS

A freely operative two-party political system has not existed in Florida since the Whig party flourished in the 1840's and 1850's. It is my purpose here to narrate the history of that party and to analyze the nature of its leadership. This is a task which would have been impossible without the innumerable courtesies of Mr. Julien C. Yonge and Mrs. Harriet Skofield of the P. K. Yonge Library of Florida History at the University of Florida, and of Mrs. Alberta Johnson of the Florida Historical Society. I am deeply appreciative of their assistance.

For constructive suggestions and criticisms in the development of this study, I am indebted to Manning J. Dauer, William G. Carleton, and Rembert W. Patrick. For wise counsel, encouragement, and stimulation, I owe much to the late Professor James Miller Leake of the University of Florida.

HERBERT J. DOHERTY, JR.

GAINESVILLE, FLORIDA
JANUARY, 1959

CONTENTS

1. EMERGENCE OF THE WHIGS

When John Branch, the last territorial governor of Florida, issued a proclamation designating May 26, 1845, as the first election day for the new state of Florida, two young political organizations readied themselves for the contest for control of the new government. The Democratic party held a convention on April 14 at Madison Court House to nominate its candidates, while Whig party leaders moved in less public and less well organized fashion to put forward their nominees.[1] Both parties, as formally organized, were scarcely six years old and had been born in the economic stresses of the years following the great nation-wide economic panic of 1837.

Though economic issues had provided the basis for party divisions, the immediate stimulus for party organization had been the summoning of a constitutional convention for the proposed state of Florida. This convention was held from December 3, 1838, to January 11, 1839, a time when the failure of the territorially backed banks was a hot issue, and the struggle between the banking and the antibanking groups in the convention over stringent regulation of corporations and government aid to them laid down lines which were to separate Democrats from Whigs for more than a decade. At the close of that convention the Democrats, who had controlled its deliberations, formally organized, though they still utilized the old terminology and styled themselves the "Jeffersonian Republican" party of Florida.[2]

The Whigs less readily adapted themselves to party organization. The groups opposing the new Democratic organization had usually controlled the government of the territory since Florida had become a United States possession, and their mode of operation was characterized by behind-the-scenes manipulation rather than by public appeals for votes. The caucus, not the convention, was their sovereign body. Informal agreements, gentlemen's understandings, and government by clique were their most familiar tools. Generally speaking, these loosely knit groups and factions were dominated by

1. *Niles' Weekly Register*, March 29, 1845.
2. St. Augustine *Florida Herald*, February 21, 1829.

the big landed interests of Florida, a lawyer-planter-speculator class whose strength was concentrated in Middle Florida, an administrative district stretching from the Apalachicola River on the west to the Suwannee River on the east. This was the early cotton-planting black belt of Florida. Through the 1820's and 1830's, as government increasingly seemed to be a monopoly of the Middle Floridians, resentment grew in extreme East and West Florida. This dominant clique soon became known as "the Nucleus," and until the panic of 1837 the territorial Legislative Council was largely under its sway. Its influence was most markedly seen in its efforts to put the encouragement of the territorial government behind the promotion of credit and transportation facilities.

Though little was done in the territorial period by way of developing transportation systems, considerable headway was made in the chartering of banks. Of the institutions established, three were most important: the Bank of Pensacola, the Union Bank of Tallahassee, and the Southern Life Insurance and Trust Company of St. Augustine.[3] Under the pressure of the propertied interests in the Legislative Council, the faith of the territory was pledged for the redemption of bonds which these three banks sold in the money markets of the world to secure their operating capital. The chief beneficiaries of the whole system were the stockholders of the banks, who had a privileged status in securing loans from them. The Union Bank was the biggest and most important, and many of its stockholders and directors were associated with the Nucleus.

In addition to its dominance in the legislature, the Nucleus controlled the governorship during much of the territorial era. William P. DuVal, governor 1822-1834, and Richard Keith Call, governor 1836-1839 and 1841-1844, were important figures in that faction. Several members of the Nucleus had been associates or cronies of Andrew Jackson, most notably Call, and they often benefited directly and indirectly from his influence. The only post of importance in Florida which was not in the hands of the Nucleus before the panic was that of delegate to Congress. This was the only post subject to election by the entire territory, and it was held from 1826 to 1838 by Joseph M. White, whose strength was based in great measure upon his reputation as an opponent of speculators and monopolists.

Even before the panic of 1837 there was evidence that the close-

3. Dorothy Dodd, *Florida Becomes a State* (Tallahassee, 1945), pp. 43-44.

knit, aristocratic Nucleus was weakening. In part the national break between the forces of Jackson and John C. Calhoun was reflected in the Nucleus, but perhaps more significant was the rapid population growth of Florida, particularly in the eastern portions where even propertied groups began to speak out against the dominance of the Middle Florida planters. The St. Augustine *Florida Herald* became the strident voice of these dissatisfied Easterners.[4]

Those who created the Florida banks, of course, expected those institutions to be beneficial to the whole community, but with the panic of 1837 they found themselves unexpectedly receiving the blame for the financial ruin which fell with impartiality on all classes. The men of the Nucleus had been so intimately tied to the banks, which received most of the blame for the depression, that they could not evade being saddled by the public with responsibility for the accumulated misfortunes of the day. Those who had long opposed the preponderance of the Nucleus in territorial government seized upon this opportunity to discredit the old leaders and to break their long dominance. In the depression which followed the panic, it was not difficult to convince the people that they had been overlooked in the distribution of the benefits, that the government which was theoretically theirs had been in the hands of a wealthy few who had used it for their own ends and to the detriment of the people. The most responsible voice of the Nucleus, the *Pensacola Gazette,* early recognized the significance of the growing antibank movement and in the fall of 1837 observed that "it is pretty evident that out of this very subject, badly understood and almost incomprehensible as it is, there are about to grow up new party distinctions."[5] As the attacks upon the bank men grew sharper and assumed a tone of class conflict, the old ruling group became more alarmed. Commented the probank paper in St. Augustine: "It is an awful struggle between virtue and corruption, and none can contemplate the consequences without the most fearful apprehensions."[6] In the face of the depression and the political storm against them the old ruling groups became confused and divided,

4. For more detailed treatment of territorial factions, see Herbert J. Doherty, Jr., "Political Factions in Territorial Florida," *Florida Historical Quarterly,* XXVIII (October, 1949), 131-142, and "Andrew Jackson's Cronies in Florida Territorial Politics," *ibid.,* XXXIV (July, 1955), 3-29.

5. October 14, 1837.   6. St. Augustine *News,* September 11, 1840.

3

some groups acquiescing in the demands for the abolition of the banks, some stubbornly standing for the banks and the repayment of their obligations whatever the cost, and some advocating preservation of the banks but repudiation or evasion of the government-endorsed bank securities.

Despite the fact that the economic issue was of overwhelming importance in drawing party lines, other political issues should be noted. National issues seem generally to have played a minor part in territorial political contests. The nullification controversy did not loom large, perhaps because Florida was not yet a state. Nullification was not endorsed by any important Florida newspaper or public man. The protective-tariff issue stirred few public utterances in the territory, but one attempt was made by Delegate White to secure tariff protection for Florida oranges.[7] Internal improvements were desired by all Floridians, and the only criticism was directed toward the fact that Florida did not get enough of them. All delegates to Congress sought federal aid for road, canal, and railroad building, as well as liberal land policies and relief from Indian troubles.[8]

Local political issues, before the financial panic of 1837, were largely centered around personalities or sectional considerations. In East Florida there was strong feeling for separation from Middle and West Florida in order to escape the dominance of the Middle Floridians and to delay the coming of statehood, which was unpopular in the East. The eruption of war with the Seminole Indians in December of 1835 and the economic distress caused by the disastrous freeze of that year strengthened East Floridians in their conviction that they could not yet bear the burdens of statehood. The antibank forces found their greatest support in East Florida, while the probank forces were strongest in Middle Florida where division of the territory was unpopular and statehood was favored. Paradoxically the antibank groups were to spearhead the statehood movement, while the conservative probank forces found themselves divided and ineffective upon that issue.

Before the panic of 1837 affected Florida, the movement for statehood had been set in motion by Governor Call's sponsorship of a referendum on the topic at the May, 1837, Congressional election.

7. *Niles' Weekly Register,* March 8, 1828.
8. James Bulger Mool, "Florida in Federal Politics: Statehood to Secession" (Master's thesis, Duke University, 1940), p. 121.

4

The results were favorable to statehood because the overwhelming majority given by Middle Florida and a good majority by West Florida overcame East Florida's substantial majority opposed to statehood.[9] Though the governor suggested a state census before calling a constitutional convention, since he feared Congress might feel Florida's population was too small to warrant admission, the territorial legislature authorized the holding of a convention in December of 1838, with the elections of convention members to be held in the preceding October. Some opposition to the convention was overcome by giving East and West Florida greater proportionate representation than Middle Florida.[10]

This convention, convening on December 3, 1838, in the midst of economic depression, furnished an admirable opportunity for the emerging Democratic party. The Florida banks had suspended specie payments in May and June of 1837.[11] By the time convention members were to be elected, it was foreseen that the territory might be called upon to make good the bonds which it had endorsed for the broken banks, and it was upon this issue that the election hinged in East Florida. Middle Florida, being more securely under the control of the bank forces, did not have this issue presented in a clear-cut fashion. It was such an important issue in the divisionist East, however, that the voters there lost sight of the fact that the antibank men whom they sent to the convention were also supporters of statehood, which most of the eastern voters opposed. The assembling convention became the arena for the struggle between the bank and antibank forces, with the controlling strength of the latter early becoming evident with the election of a presiding officer. David Levy, an antibank leader from St. Augustine, had looked to this contest as a test of strength between the rival economic forces, but this it was only indirectly, since sectional biases also played a part. The antibank candidate, Robert Raymond Reid of St. Augustine, defeated the probank candidate, William P. DuVal, by a single vote. Greater majorities were later secured for articles restricting the banks. Levy more correctly observed that the actions which the convention took toward deciding the fate of the banking institutions would decide the fate of the two parties.[12]

9. Dodd, pp. 34, 37-38.   10. Dodd, pp. 38-39.
11. *Pensacola Gazette*, May 13, June 10, 1837.
12. *Journal of the Proceedings of a Convention of Delegates to Form*

Despite the defeat of attempts by the more radical antibank forces, led by Levy, to use the convention to intervene actively in territorial affairs and to repudiate the "faith bonds," the record of the convention was clearly antibank. Under the leadership of Thomas Baltzell, a Jackson County antibank man, it petitioned Congress to interpose its power to modify or repeal the corporation charters granted by the territory. The convention approved this petition 38 to 18 despite bitter opposition. Edward C. Cabell, later a Whig congressman, insisted that the petition transcended the power of the convention and contained loose and unfounded allegations intended to create public excitement.[13]

From the convention's committee on banking came the recommendation for an article restricting the life and activities of any corporations created by the state, forbidding the state to pledge its credit to the support of any corporation, and depriving bank officials of the right to hold public office. This committee was headed by an aggressive, ardent antibank man from Middle Florida, James D. Westcott. Levy, Reid, and Westcott constituted a triumvirate which came virtually to dominate the new Democratic party. The bank men deeply resented Westcott's activities, and DuVal on one occasion sarcastically thanked him for "his universal action and unlimited efforts to conduct the entire business of this body."[14] Though the antibank forces did not secure everything they wished from the convention, the restrictions upon banks which were written into the new constitution amounted to a substantial victory for their cause. This success had been largely built upon the cooperation of the East Florida delegation headed by Levy and Reid with the Middle and West Florida antibank men led by Westcott.[15]

On the opposing side in the convention were found many able men who later were Whigs and most of whom had earlier been identified with the Nucleus. Among them the most prominent were George T. Ward, Thomas Brown, William P. DuVal of Leon

a Constitution for the People of Florida (St. Joseph, 1839), p. 7; F. W. Hoskins, "The St. Joseph Convention," Florida Historical Quarterly, XVI (October, 1937), 107-108.

13. Convention Journal, pp. 41, 73-74, 116-117.

14. James Owen Knauss, Territorial Florida Journalism (DeLand, 1926), p. 185.

15. For a detailed treatment of the constitutional convention, see Dodd, pp. 47-66.

County, and Edward C. Cabell of Jefferson County. The two opposing factions were not so sharply divided on other issues, most notably apportionment of seats in the state legislature. On that question Westcott abandoned his Eastern friends, with the result that they were disappointed in the allotment of seats to their section.[16]

The members of the antibank majority in the convention, however, impressed with the success which they had secured by organized action, determined to consolidate their position in order to wield power in territorial politics, as well as in the future new state. For these reasons their meeting already referred to was held in St. Joseph after the close of the convention on January 11, 1839, and the "Jeffersonian Republican" party was formally called into existence. Party officers were named from all sections of Florida, well-turned resolutions were adopted in praise of the Jeffersonian Republican faith, adherence to the Van Buren administration was proclaimed, and committees of correspondence in every county were planned.[17] Increasingly after the convention the groups in opposition to the Democrats were called Whigs, although they themselves were slow to adopt the name and were even slower to form an effective organization. They had contemptuously dubbed the Democrats "locofocos" during the convention, but they had little success in making that term stick as a popular label in Florida.

In the 1838 elections success rewarded Democratic efforts to win control of the lower house of the Legislative Council, and the Democratic constitution was narrowly approved by the voters. In the race for delegate to Congress, however, Thomas Baltzell, a Middle Florida Democrat, was defeated by antistatehood, probank Charles Downing of East Florida. A sectional disruption among the Democrats seems to explain this. East Floridians were rankled about the apportionment of legislative seats in the new constitution, though many Democrats claimed with David Levy that they had not supported Baltzell because they were not convinced that he was a true antibank man.[18]

Late in 1839 the Democrats secured a triumph of major pro-

16. Dodd, pp. 60, 320-321. West Florida received 14 seats, Middle Florida got 24, and East Florida was allotted 20.
17. Dodd, pp. 334-335.
18. St. Augustine *Florida Herald,* January 9, 1840; St. Augustine *News,* May 11, 1839; Dodd, p. 71.

portions in getting President Van Buren to remove Richard K. Call from the governorship and to replace him with Robert Raymond Reid. Call had done much to make himself unpopular in Washington. He had long been critical of the Van Buren wing of the Democrats, and he had been a bitter critic of the policies followed by the Van Buren administration in prosecuting the war against the Florida Indians.[19] More recently Call had wearied the President with incessant demands that the territorial secretary be dismissed. John P. DuVal, a Democrat and a brother of former Governor DuVal, held this post and was frequently absent from Florida for months at a time on personal business.[20] These facts, plus Call's favoritism to the probank people, served to make him even more unpopular among local Democrats than in Washington, and Reid and Levy undertook a campaign to discredit the governor and effect his removal. One important document in this campaign was an able analysis of the political scene in Florida which Levy sent to Van Buren in 1839. In it he urged that the government be placed in "thoroughly democratic hands," and added, *"I can satisfy the administration* that it [the governorship] is not now in hands at all likely to *advocate or advance its interests* or to uphold the democratic movements."[21]

The decisive influence in Call's removal, however, seems to have been a letter to the President by Secretary of War Joel R. Poinsett in November, 1839. Poinsett had long been upset by Call's criticisms of War Department policies in the Florida Indian war and had been goaded by Levy and Reid to ask Call's removal. This he finally did, citing disagreements on military policy as the grounds for removal. Improvement could not be expected in Florida affairs, he warned, "so long as the present Governor remains in power." Martin Van Buren approved of this sentiment and scrawled on the

19. St. Augustine *News*, December 8, 1838, July 31, 1840. For details of Call's participation in the Indian war, see Herbert J. Doherty, Jr., "R. K. Call *vs.* the Federal Government on the Seminole War," *Florida Historical Quarterly*, XXXI (January, 1953), 163-180.

20. R. K. Call to John Forsyth, June 3, 1837, June [?], 1839, "Miscellaneous Letters Received," State Department; Call to Martin Van Buren, November 24, 1839, "Miscellaneous Letters Received," State Department, National Archives.

21. David Levy, "Brief remarks concerning the Democratic cause in Florida, with a suggestion, respectfully submitted to the President," Van Buren papers, Library of Congress.

back of the letter: "Let Gov. Call be superceded [sic] & Judge Reid appointed in his place."[22]

Call was an ardent, volatile man and he made a public issue of his removal, charging that the President masked political motives with military policy statements. He ridiculed Poinsett and Van Buren and charged that "the petty corporations of this Territory have claimed more paternal concern from the Federal Executive than the Seminole War which is depopulating the country, consuming the substance of our people, and draining the last artery of the national Treasury."[23] The Whig newspapers echoed Call's bitterness toward the Democrats, and the former governor, in a spirit of revenge, endorsed William H. Harrison for the presidency and did yeoman service for the Whig cause in the 1840 presidential canvass.

In the territorial elections of 1840 a lack of unity among the Whigs was made obvious by their factionalism. The opposition to the Democrats in Middle Florida was divided between "State Rights" Whigs and Conservatives. The Conservative party was sometimes referred to as the "Federal" Whig party, but its members were bound together only in their adherence to the banks, and not all of them were Whigs. It included William P. DuVal, Brown, Ward, and other stalwarts of the old Nucleus who stood firm for the banks, but it also included such probank Democrats as Benjamin F. Whitner, Charles H. Dupont, and Leslie A. Thompson. Indeed, by 1848 DuVal himself was in Democratic ranks.[24]

By contrast, the State Rights Whigs were realistic enough to see that the banks could not be revived and that no political capital could be made by insisting that they ought to be. Though the members of this faction would not repudiate just debts or impair the obligations of proper contracts, they rather speciously argued that the territorial government had not possessed the power to charter banks or pledge its credit to them. William Wyatt was the main spokesman for this viewpoint, and the *Florida Sentinel* was the organ of the faction.[25]

Though the groups maintained separate organizations, neither in

22. Joel R. Poinsett to Van Buren, November 29, 1839, Van Buren papers.
23. "Memorial of Richard K. Call," *House Executive Documents,* 26 Congress, 1 Session, No. 136, pp. 13-14.
24. Tallahassee *Floridian,* September 5, 1840; Tallahassee *Star of Florida,* August 18, 1841; Marianna *Florida Whig,* April 5, 1848.
25. Tallahassee *Florida Sentinel,* September 17, 1841.

9

the 1840 election nor in that of 1841 did Whig candidates appear on the ballot to weaken the Conservatives. After 1841 the Conservatives disappeared, and their newspaper, the *Star of Florida,* tended toward an independent course, though inclined toward the Whigs. The temporary alliance of Whigs and Democrats under the Conservative label to support local banks was not a development peculiar to Florida. Most scholars have noted similar movements in Virginia under William C. Rives and in New York under Nathaniel P. Tallmadge, though there were also similar movements throughout the Union. Such men as William L. May of Illinois, Josiah Caldwell of Massachusetts, and John Ruggles and George Evans of Maine were prominent in their leadership.[26]

In East Florida during the years after the panic of 1837 organized opposition to the antibank forces had been growing, but had lacked ties with the Middle Florida groups and had often worked at cross-purposes with them. In 1838 a probank newspaper, *The News,* was established in St. Augustine and led the opposition to the Levy-Reid faction. In the late 1830's those who later were to be the East Florida Whigs appeared before the electorate as the People's party, and in 1840 they proclaimed themselves the "True Democratic Republican" ticket. After 1840 the *News,* and presumably its backers, accepted the Whig label.[27] In West Florida party spirit was remarkably lacking, and bipartisan cooperation was frequent through the territorial period, despite the presence of the pro-Whig *Pensacola Gazette* under the able guidance of its editor Benjamin D. Wright.

Having retained control of the lower house of the Legislative Council in 1840, and still riding on the steam generated by the bank and bond controversy, the Democrats entered the 1841 elections with the added advantage that the foreign bondholders of the Florida banks were pressing the governor for payment of the interest in default on the bonds of the Bank of Pensacola.[28] This resulted in a more sweeping Democratic victory in the house of the Legislative Council. The Democrats and antibank Whigs controlled the

26. Wilfred E. Binkley, *American Political Parties* (New York, 1947), p. 161; Henry H. Simms, *The Rise of the Whigs in Virginia* (Richmond, 1929), p. 127; William G. Carleton, "Political Aspects of the Van Buren Era," *South Atlantic Quarterly,* L (April, 1951), 168.
27. St. Augustine *News,* December 8, 1838, July 31, October 23, 1840.
28. Dodd, p. 77.

senate.[29] The race for delegate to Congress was marked this time by an East-West rift among the Whigs and by unity among the Democrats. Since December, 1840, the Conservative organ in Tallahassee had been highly critical of Downing, who by this time had completely alienated West and Middle Florida by his inconsistent stand on statehood, a stand which was ultimately climaxed by his flat opposition to it. Besides, he had accomplished little for Florida in his second term and was under fire in East Florida on that score.[30] Consequently the Middle Florida Conservatives put forth an outspoken defender of the banks, George T. Ward, as their candidate. State Rights Whigs were silent on his candidacy, though many evidently did not support him. For himself Ward asserted that he was an old Whig and not a new recruit. Even after he had been put forward for Congress, Ward had offered to let a convention choose between himself and Downing, but Downing refused and insisted upon running. The Democrats, in a show of unity, named David Levy as their candidate. His strength among the antibank forces of Middle Florida, along with his East Florida following, gave him the victory at the election of May, 1841, although the combined vote of his two opponents was about 500 greater than his.[31]

Yet all was not dark for the Whigs in 1841, for the victorious Whig presidential candidate had been inaugurated on March 4. Charles Downing, the territorial delegate to Congress, had immediately pressed upon the old general the claims of Call to the governorship, fearing efforts made by William Wyatt to get the post. Only four days after the inauguration Downing excitedly dashed off a note to Call, saying: "I have seen old Tip, & he says you shall be Gov."[32] It is well that he acted as hastily as he did, for less than four weeks later, exhausted by office seekers, the old President was dead. By early April, Call had been reinstated as governor and remained in that post until the expiration of his term in 1844.

29. Tallahassee *Florida Sentinel*, October 22, 1841; Tallahassee *Star of Florida*, January 7, February 10, 1842.
30. Tallahassee *Star of Florida*, December 19, 1840; Dodd, p. 76.
31. Tallahassee *Florida Sentinel*, May 21, 1841; Tallahassee *Floridian*, June 18, 1841.
32. Charles Downing to R. K. Call, March 8, 1841, Call papers, Florida Historical Society Library.

During 1842 the strongly antibank Legislative Council moved to settle the bank-bond issue once and for all. Though Call did not believe that the "faith bonds" should be repudiated, he believed that the stockholders of the banks were unlimitedly liable and that the territory bore no responsibility for payment until they had individually been prosecuted into insolvency by the bondholders, a prospect for which the bondholders had no relish. This stand undoubtedly cost Call support among the probank groups who held stock. Call himself was one of the few members of the old Nucleus who owned no bank stock. Brushing aside the Whig governor's views, the legislators repudiated all territorial responsibility for the bonds and passed acts calling for the cancellation of the bonds and forbidding the issuance of more. These acts were passed over the governor's veto.[33] The 1842 Legislative Council took further notice of the financial depression, which still dragged on, by indefinitely suspending the collection of taxes. A stay law was approved prohibiting the sale of property under execution, providing a small payment could be made toward the judgment every sixty days. Resolutions were also adopted urging the delegate to Congress to press for Florida's early admission to the Union.[34]

Apparently the actions of the Legislative Council of 1842 worked against the Democrats, perhaps because the repudiation of the bonds took much of the popular appeal from the bank-bond issue. As hard times persisted, the Whigs pointed out that Democratic measures had not solved the people's economic troubles, and called for governmental and monetary reforms.[35] At the October, 1842, election the Whigs won control of both houses of the Council and repeated their victory in the fall of 1843. It should be pointed out that the Whigs did not regain control of the Council because of the revalidation of their old principles, rather it was a result of the modification of Whig ideas to bring them closer to those of the Democrats. It was accepted that the banks could not be saved and that the "faith bonds" never would be paid.

The Whigs also learned much from the Democrats about party organization. Whig newspapers berated Westcott as an absolute

33. Florida *House Journal* (1842), pp. 17-18, 19-20; *Acts and Resolutions of the Legislative Council* (1842), pp. 45, 53.
34. *Acts and Resolutions* (1842), pp. 22, 54, 55-56.
35. Tallahassee *Florida Sentinel,* September 2, 30, 1842.

ruler of the Democrats, but admitted that the Whigs would do well to copy his organizational methods. The *Florida Sentinel* complained: "While the Whigs have suffered themselves to fall into disorganization and sundered party ties, by personal disputes, doubts, and recriminations . . . the little knot of Locofoco managers have been industriously at work in strengthening their cords, and will bind us hand and foot unless we make a Sampson-like struggle for ourselves."[36] Copying Democratic techniques, the Whigs soon were forming county organizations and using conventions both at the county and district levels for the nomination of candidates.[37]

The two Whig-controlled Councils elected in 1842 and 1843 convened respectively in 1843 and 1844, and the problems with which they had to deal were largely financial in nature. New tax laws had to be passed, and there was still pressure from Middle Florida for the creation of new credit facilities. Most Whigs, however, were reluctant to risk party fortunes on more banking experiments, and no new institutions were chartered. On financial grounds the question of statehood was again revived by the Easterners who opposed it. Isaiah D. Hart, a Whig senator from Duval County, introduced resolutions which would have nullified the St. Joseph convention and would have required the delegate to Congress to oppose Florida's admission until a new convention should be held. The major argument in support of this move was that the people could not bear the financial burdens of statehood. Although Hart's resolutions failed of passage, the Council did pass substitute resolutions declaring it unwise to enter into statehood at that time and instructing the delegate to oppose statehood until a new convention had been held or the people had approved the St. Joseph constitution in a new referendum.[38] In the 1844 session the anti-statehood forces were powerful enough to secure the passage of resolutions calling for the division of Florida into two territories with separate governments. Congress turned down this request, but notice was taken of preparations for a constitutional convention in Iowa territory, and all actions on Florida's admission were postponed

36. August 12, 1842.
37. Tallahassee *Florida Sentinel,* July 18, 1843; Tallahassee *Star of Florida,* August 16, 30, 1844.
38. Florida *Senate Journal* (1843), pp. 53-54; *Acts and Resolutions* (1843), p. 66.

until Iowa's application should be received.[39] Thus, while avoiding further favoritism to banks, the Whigs in these sessions had become identified with the antistatehood forces.

David Levy was re-elected to Congress in 1843, despite the uniting of the Whigs behind George T. Ward, and Levy promptly took upon himself the task of readying his constituents for statehood. Always a quiet advocate of statehood, he now became its loudest champion. One important argument which he advanced was the necessity of Florida entering the Union to balance Iowa and preserve the political equality of the South with the North. He also emphasized that statehood would mean freedom from federal interference, the election of all governing officers, and a greater voice in national politics. He admitted that statehood would entail responsibilities and some sacrifices, but he effectively minimized what the burdens might mean to individuals. This initiative from an outstanding Democrat was instrumental in crediting his party with the statehood movement. Levy was so effective that a Democratic Legislative Council was elected in 1844 to renew Florida's application for admission.[40]

Despite the fact that the Democratic Legislative Council meeting in 1845 renewed Florida's application for statehood, over the objections of a few Whigs from East and West Florida, Congress had not waited for this action. The Committee on Territories of the House of Representatives reported a bill on January 7, 1845, for the admission of both Florida and Iowa. It passed the House on February 13, was approved by the Senate on March 1, and was signed by the President on March 3.[41] Governor Call's term had expired in July of 1844, and President John Tyler had replaced him with John Branch, a Democrat. Thus it was that the transition to statehood was made completely under Democratic auspices.

Though the Democrats held a state-wide convention at Madison on April 14, 1845, to name their slate of candidates for the officers of the new state government, the Whigs proceeded through a caucus of the Whig members of the Legislative Council. These gentlemen hoped to find a candidate pleasing to both parties who might run

39. Dodd, pp. 82-83; *Acts and Resolutions* (1844), pp. 95-96.
40. St. Augustine *Florida Herald*, October 22, 29, November 5, 1844; Dodd, p. 84.
41. *Niles' Weekly Register*, March 29, 1845; Dodd, pp. 85-86.

on a nonpartisan basis. They selected William Bailey, a wealthy planter of Jefferson County and a Democrat, but he rebuffed their overtures, saying that he would welcome Whig support if the Democrats should nominate him. The Democrats were in no mood to talk of nonpartisanship, however, and turned away from Bailey early in their convention to give the gubernatorial nomination to William D. Moseley of Leon County and the Congressional nomination to David Levy. Levy, however, would accept the nomination only with the understanding that he should be elected United States Senator if the Democrats should win the legislature.[42]

At the close of the Democrats' convention the Whigs still had no candidates. The caucus of Council members had earlier named Joseph B. Lancaster of Duval County for Congress, but Whig meetings in East Florida were advocating Benjamin Putnam of St. Johns County. There was not time for a convention to be summoned, so Middle Florida Whigs acted to bring some semblance of organization to party ranks. Whig leaders from Leon, Wakulla, and Gadsden counties met at the Leon County courthouse on April 22 and unanimously nominated Richard Keith Call for the governorship. To placate the East, Benjamin Putnam was endorsed for Congress. This group noted that they acted only because the "emergency" necessitated some move on behalf of the entire party.[43]

Though the campaign of 1845 was a hot one, it marked one of the lowest ebbs of the Whigs' strength before their great triumph of 1848. In addition to their hesitancy over candidates and their bumbling party organization, the Whigs were losing newspaper strength. The Tallahassee *Star of Florida*, which had been the voice of the Conservative party and had usually favored the Whigs, turned to neutrality in a "plague on both your houses" manner. The only Whig bulwark in the East, the St. Augustine *News*, was purchased from its Whig editor, Thomas T. Russell, by Albert A. Nunes who carried it over to the Democratic ranks. Its retiring editor lamented: "An able paper or a useful paper must have support." Though the *Star* did not advocate the Democrats, it saw little hope that Moseley could be defeated, and it set down the election of Levy

42. *Niles' Weekly Register*, March 29, 1845; *Pensacola Gazette*, May 3, 1845; Tallahassee *Florida Sentinel*, May 3, 1845; Dodd, pp. 87-88.

43 St. Augustine *News*, February 8, 1845; *Pensacola Gazette*, May 3, 1845.

as certain.[44] Only the *Pensacola Gazette* and the Tallahassee *Florida Sentinel* remained to serve the Whigs in 1845.

In the campaign neither party presented much in the way of a program. The Whigs were attacked for their former connection with the banks and the "faith bonds" and for their opposition to statehood. Whigs charged the Democrats with being political spoilsmen and machine politicians who dictated to the people. Since neither Moseley nor Putnam were widely known, the burden of the campaign was carried by Call and Levy, who attacked each other as ferociously as if they were contending for the same office. The past records of both the parties and their candidates were the major issues. Generally the constructive side of the Whig arguments stressed unity, efficiency in government, and the subordination of partisan politics to the welfare of the new state. The Whig campaign was eminently unsuccessful, and at the May 26 election the Democrats won the governorship, the Congressional seat, and both houses of the General Assembly. In the senate the Whigs won but six seats in a total of seventeen, and in the house ten in a total of forty. Thomas Brown was the only notable Whig representative, and David S. Walker and Benjamin D. Wright were the most prominent Whig senators. In the state-wide races the high man was Levy with 3,614 votes, then Moseley with 3,292. Call drew 2,679 votes for governor which put him 284 votes ahead of his running mate Putnam.[45] Call and Putnam together had majorities only in the West Florida counties of Escambia, Santa Rosa, Walton, and Jackson, counties which were to be Whig strongholds throughout the life of the party.

The first General Assembly convened on June 23 and, controlling it, the Democrats were to choose Florida's first two United States Senators. David Levy and James D. Westcott, virtually unchallenged leaders of the party since the death of Robert Raymond Reid in 1841, were elected by a strict party vote on July 1. Their Whig opponents were Jackson Morton of Pensacola and Joseph M. Hernandez of St. Augustine, each of whom was defeated by a 41 to 16 vote. The two Whig newspapers, in the face of the enormous

44. St. Augustine *News*, April 12, 1845; Tallahassee *Star of Florida*, April 18, 1845.

45. St. Augustine *Florida Herald*, May 6, 20, 1845; St. Augustine *News*, April 26, 1845.

Democratic success, contented themselves with attempts to divide Levy and Westcott. The *Pensacola Gazette* ran a sarcastic letter paying tribute to Westcott as one who ran the Democrats as completely "as the autocrat of Russia rules his dominions. . . . The titulary authorities of the state are but puppets in his hands and organs of his will; they live by his permission and reign through his power."[46] The *Florida Sentinel* consoled the friends of Levy that there had not been offices enough for the friends of both the Democratic bosses. Levy, the *Sentinel* said, was lucky to have come off with an office for himself. That the Whigs may not have been on a wild-goose chase is suggested by the fact that the *Southern Journal,* a Democratic paper, was set up in 1846 in Tallahassee in competition with the old Democratic organ, the *Floridian.* The *Journal* spoke highly of Levy. A battle between the two top Democrats never came off, however. Westcott was content to fade from active politics after his senatorial term, leaving Levy the unquestioned senior Democrat.[47]

46. July 12, 26, 1845.
47. Tallahassee *Florida Sentinel,* February 3, 1846. See also Tallahassee *Southern Journal,* January, February, and March, 1846.

2. THE RISE TO POWER

The election of Levy, or David Levy Yulee as he now called himself, to the United States Senate vacated Florida's seat in the House of Representatives. The vacancy was to be filled at a special election in October, 1845. The Whigs were understandably apathetic about running a candidate so soon after their crushing defeat, and Benjamin D. Wright expressed in his *Pensacola Gazette* the view that it would be best for the Whigs to pass up the race. Into this gloomy picture, however, strode the vigorous young Edward C. Cabell, who had completed his law training at the University of Virginia since taking part as a fledgling politician in the St. Joseph convention. Only twenty-nine years old, an excellent though not flamboyant speaker, practically a newcomer on the political scene, he undoubtedly brought a breath of fresh air into Florida politics and new hope to the Whigs. Declaring himself the Whig candidate for the House of Representatives, he proceeded to rejuvenate his party. The *Gazette* seemed startled that anyone should be "willing to lead the forlorn hope," but endorsed young Cabell, saying: "It shall not be ours to discourage any who may choose to do battle with him and strike once more for the good old conservative cause of the Whigs."[1]

To oppose Cabell the Democrats named William H. Brockenbrough, a former member of the territorial legislature. Many Democrats viewed him with suspicion, and he seems to have been an unfortunate choice. He was reported to have been a Harrison supporter in 1840 and probably had been a member of the old Conservative party. A letter signed "Democrat" appeared in the neutral *Star*, saying: "In the present juncture of affairs, a Democrat may consistently give him [Cabell] his support." It must have seemed odd to the electorate that the Democrats did not again ride the bank and bond issue in this race, as they had in earlier ones. The *Gazette* took this as evidence that the issue had about played out; however, it would have been difficult to connect Cabell intimately with the banks or the "faith bonds" because of his youth and previous lack of involvement in politics. Cabell was by no

1. August 16, 1845.

18

means a doctrinaire Whig, and he refused to let his opponent place him in the position of advocating the payment of the repudiated bonds.[2]

As the official returns from the election came in, an extremely tight race was indicated. By law all county returns had to be submitted by judges of probate to the secretary of state within thirty days after the election. At that date Cabell had won a majority in the returns received by that official, who duly certified his election to the Democratic governor, and the latter in turn issued Cabell a commission as Florida's duly elected Representative. The supporters of Brockenbrough were loud in their protests that all the returns were not in and that their candidate would have a majority when all the votes should be counted. The hesitancy of the Whig press about the soundness of Cabell's case seems an indication that claims of the Democrats were well founded. At any rate, Brockenbrough contested Cabell's election. In the contest he argued that Cabell had not received a majority of all the votes cast and that because returns had been made by unauthorized persons, a majority of the votes legally returned was in his favor even at the time the commission was issued to Cabell. Though Cabell had already been seated, the House Committee on Elections upheld Brockenbrough's argument that only judges of probate were authorized to make returns and ruled out all returns made by county clerks, leaving Brockenbrough with a majority of 114. The committee further pointed out that if late returns were counted, Brockenbrough's majority would be 169. On this evidence the committee recommended unseating Cabell in favor of Brockenbrough, and the House upheld the recommendation.[3]

Most Whigs, agreeing with the Apalachicola paper, seemed to think that Cabell had been cheated and that "he owes his defeat solely to the influence of party drill." The *Pensacola Gazette*, however, refused to shed tears over his ejection from the House. It pointed out that who got the seat was not important; what mattered

2. Apalachicola *Commercial Advertiser*, May 9, 1846; *Pensacola Gazette*, August 16, 1845.
3. Tallahassee *Star of Florida*, November 14, 1845; *Niles' Weekly Register*, November 22, 1845; Tallahassee *Florida Sentinel*, December 2, 1845; U. S. House of Representatives, *Reports of Committees*, 29 Congress, 1 Session, No. 35; *Journal of the House of Representatives of the United States*, 29 Congress, 1 Session, pp. 295-296.

was the fact that the Whig party had found good heart for the struggle again.[4]

Since the contested term expired in 1846, the Congressional campaign apparently never stopped between the 1845 and 1846 elections. The biggest issue in 1846 was Cabell's loss of his seat. He claimed that Brockenbrough had usurped the right to represent Florida and that the Democrats had been forced to get their party in Congress to do for them "what the people of Florida refused to do."[5] Whig papers took up the cry, and everywhere Cabell was painted as one sorely wronged by party machination. Such a man, said one, "may be forced into retirement by the unjust decision of a party majority, but he cannot be kept there."[6] Not to his party, but to his own efforts, did Cabell owe his growing strength. Diligently he took to the stump and as the *Florida Herald* noted, "perambulated the State" to organize a party. He did not allow the Democrats to tie him to old issues, and he represented himself as one of the people in terms which would have done credit to the most rabid Democrat. His efforts probably more than those of any other single man brought the Whig party through one of its darkest periods, and in the doing Edward C. Cabell proved himself the most skilled practical politician among the Florida Whigs.[7]

The Democrats countered Cabell's campaign with charges that he stood on no principles, that he merely cried about being unseated in Congress. In an attempt to kill the contested election as an issue, the Democratic state convention denied renomination to Brockenbrough and named little-known William A. Kain, a state senator and merchant from Apalachicola. Again, however, the Democrats seem to have chosen a weak candidate, and the heartened Whig forces closed in for the kill. In addition to charging Democrats with the theft of the last Congressional race, the Whigs saddled them with charges of extravagance in running the state government. In their exuberant campaign for statehood the sanguine Democrats had generally underestimated the costs of state government and the

---

4. Apalachicola *Commercial Advertiser*, February 14, 1846; *Pensacola Gazette*, December 13, 1845.

5. E. C. Cabell to Joseph Clisby, January 24, 1846, in Tallahassee *Florida Sentinel*, February 10, 1846.

6. Apalachicola *Commercial Advertiser*, April 25, 1846.

7. St. Augustine *Florida Herald*, June 16, 1846; Palatka *Whig Banner*, July 7, 28, 1846.

Whigs now gleefully contrasted the earlier estimates with the actual costs. Criticism was also leveled at the Democrats for *not* winding up the affairs of the local banks as rapidly as they had pledged to do. The state constitution, said the Whigs, vested in the General Assembly the power to regulate banks, and the Democratic Assembly had failed to use this power to complete the liquidation of the territorial banks, thereby violating solemn pledges. On national issues Cabell declared himself at odds with state-rights extremists among the Democrats and linked them with the old Federalists who had talked of secession in the War of 1812. He declared that he favored a tariff for revenue with incidental protection.[8]

Cabell narrowly defeated Kain (2,978 to 2,885) in 1846, but with this election the reaction against the Democratic party began to grow. Though the Democrats still controlled the General Assembly, the Whigs made heartening gains. The senate divided at seven Whigs and twelve Democrats, while the house had seventeen Whigs and twenty-two Democrats.[9] The reasons for this reaction can be traced to both local and national developments.

On the local scene the banking issue was fading, and there was a tendency to forget the financial panic of 1837, now almost ten years in the past. Too, the constitution of 1839, written by Democrats in the heat of the panic, was appearing to more and more men to be a hindrance with its restrictions on corporations. Projects for cotton mills, canals, plank roads, and railroads were filling men's minds, and not only were credit facilities needed for these, but state aid could be beneficial were it not for the restrictions of the constitution. Even the anticlerical provision which barred ministers from holding high political office was being turned against the Democrats. The Whigs criticized, too, the Democrats' convention system, terming it "prone to destroy the spirit of our institutions." Furthermore, the bargain by which Yulee became Senator and the unseating of Cabell were cited as proofs that the Democrats were not at all reluctant to pervert the will of the people.[10]

There were many persons among the Whigs at this time who

8. St. Augustine *Florida Herald,* August 11, 1846; Tallahassee *Florida Sentinel,* July 21, August 11, 18, 1846.
9. *Niles' Weekly Register,* December 5, 1846; St. Augustine *News,* November 13, 1846.
10. Tallahassee *Florida Sentinel,* April 14, 1846; Palatka *Whig Banner,* July 28, 1846.

also feared that the Democrats were too radical on national issues. Though the annexation of Texas and the war with Mexico had not been important political issues in Florida, many Whigs privately opposed them and were disturbed by the annexationist spirit of the Polk administration. When before being in the Senate a month, Yulee introduced a resolution looking to the annexation of Cuba, such men were horrified. The act met with severe criticism, and the *Pensacola Gazette* in consternation termed the move indelicate, improper, and impolitic.[11] The Mexican War had been productive of the Wilmot Proviso, an attempt to close to slavery the territory acquired from Mexico, which squarely and explicitly laid the slavery-antislavery issue before the country. Whigs had feared such a consequence of annexationist policies and generally sought to suppress sectional agitation, while Southern expansionists and extreme pro-slavery men had more and more attached themselves to the Democratic party.[12] The dominant interests of the national Whig party—industrialists, common carriers, financiers, Ohio Valley farmers, Southern planters—"all dependent more or less on the slave economy of the Southern plantation," dreaded agitation of the slavery question and were the forces which maintained the officially moderate position of the national Whig party as long as they were able.[13]

Whether Whigs or Democrats, Floridians were in agreement on certain basic principles at this time. These principles were the right to carry property, in this case slaves, into the nation's territories and to maintain the institution of slavery where it already existed. The main difference between Democrats and Whigs was the extent to which these rights should be insisted upon. The Whigs were less inclined to force the issue than were the Democrats, and were more disposed to compromise on the extension of slavery to the territories. Yet even before 1850 there was a free-soil element among the Northern Whigs which troubled Southerners.[14]

After Cabell's election in Florida local Democrats tried to enlarge

11. January 10, 1846; see also *Niles' Weekly Register*, December 27, 1845; and William T. Cash, *History of the Democratic Party in Florida* (Tallahassee, 1936), p. 26.

12. Ulrich B. Phillips, "The Southern Whigs," *Essays in American History* (New York, 1910), p. 219.

13. Wilfred C. Binkley, *American Political Parties* (New York, 1947), p. 177.

14. Arthur C. Cole, *The Whig Party in the South* (Washington, 1913), p. 123.

22

upon the differences between Northern and Southern Whigs and to paint the latter as subordinate to the former. The St. Augustine *News* said of Cabell: "The Abolition Whigs now claim him as their own, and struggle as he will, he is now bound to them hand and foot by the ties of party."[15] The Whigs, on the other hand, emphasized their moderation and conservatism. Cabell attacked sectional viewpoints, declaring that the Whig party "embraced in its comprehensive view the whole country. It is not influenced by a narrow, contracted sectional policy."[16] Many Northern Whigs made great efforts to conciliate the South; Henry Clay expressed a willingness to compromise his tariff views, and Daniel Webster thundered against the abolitionists.[17]

Many Democrats were in sympathy with efforts to minimize sectionalism at this time. Florida's Senator Westcott was unwilling to advocate extreme state-rights ideas and joined with Cabell in refusing to sign the "Southern Address" which Calhoun prepared during the Thirtieth Congress and which demanded the suppression of abolition activity and asked for unrestricted slavery in all territories. Westcott objected that it contained "no declaration of the attachment of the South to the Constitution and to the Union."[18] Yulee signed the declaration. The extremism of the Democrats and the professed conservatism of the Whigs, North and South, apparently worked to the benefit of the Whigs in the late 1840's.

In the state elections of October, 1847, the Whig party won control of both houses of the General Assembly.[19] The local issues had revolved around a proposed amendment to the state constitution to make Assembly elections and sessions biennial and around the question of the payment of jurors. Both parties favored the amendment, but Governor Moseley had vetoed a bill for payment of jurors and the Whigs had campaigned for such payment. Controlling both houses, the Whigs organized them along strict party lines, to the disgust of Democrats who had been the targets of Whig criticisms for doing the same thing. Daniel G. McLean of Walton

15. November 13, 1846. 16. Marianna *Florida Whig,* February 9, 1848.
17. Charles S. Sydnor, *The Development of Southern Sectionalism, 1819-1848* (Baton Rouge, 1948), p. 319; Arthur M. Schlesinger, Jr., *The Age of Jackson* (Boston, 1947), p. 371.
18. James Bulger Mool, "Florida in Federal Politics" (Master's thesis, Duke University, 1940), p. 46.
19. Tallahassee *Florida Sentinel,* October 19, 1847.

County became president of the senate, while Charles W. Downing, son of the late territorial delegate, was named secretary. Joseph B. Lancaster of Duval County became speaker of the house and Wilkinson Call, youthful nephew of former territorial Governor Richard K. Call, was named clerk.[20]

The Whig-controlled General Assembly concerned itself in 1848 to some extent with the promotion of conditions favorable to business and industry in Florida. By this time the Democrats were mellowing in their radicalism toward corporations and government aid to them. In 1844 Yulee had suggested that a cross-state railroad be built by the new state government so that the people could avoid the "impositions and exactions which a private chartered monopoly would impose."[21] After statehood was accomplished, however, talk of government ownership diminished, though Yulee and others continued to agitate for a cross-state railway. In the 1848 legislature the House Committee on Internal Improvements recommended action looking toward such railroad construction. It urged that one-half million acres of land donated by Congress for internal improvements be used in furthering such a road, and it recommended that the Assembly "hold out inducements to companies to subscribe the balance of the stock." In 1848, however, financial conditions still seemed unfavorable for action of this sort, and such a road was not chartered until the next session.[22]

More important political news was being made outside the legislature, however, where public meetings, caucuses, and party newspapers were whipping up the partisan fervor of a presidential election year. This was a new experience to Floridians, who had never had a vote in presidential contests before. There was considerable feeling, mostly in West Florida and among the older Whigs, that Henry Clay should be the party nominee. Jackson County Whigs endorsed Clay and approved resolutions condemning the Wilmot Proviso, criticizing the Mexican War as one of conquest, opposing the annexation of Mexican territory, and praising both

20. *Pensacola Gazette,* December 4, 1847.
21. David Levy, *Circular Letter to the People of Florida Relative to the Admission of Florida Into the Union* (n.p., 1844), P. K. Yonge Library of Florida History, University of Florida.
22. Marianna *Florida Whig,* January 5, 1848; Arthur W. Thompson, "The Railroad Background of the Florida Senatorial Election of 1851," *Florida Historical Quarterly,* XXXI (January, 1953), 184-185.

Zachary Taylor and Winfield Scott for their military exploits.[23] In Middle and East Florida, and among younger men, General Zachary Taylor, the hero of the Mexican War, was favored.

Only a month after the Jackson County meeting Peter Sken Smith, a St. Augustine Whig, released to the Whig press of the state a letter from Taylor which was intended to convey Taylor's willingness to be president, but which revealed a lack of real political interests or beliefs on his part. In the letter Taylor stated principles later embodied in the famous "Allison letter" which got national circulation, but he was not sufficiently attached to the Whig cause in the Smith letter. In the latter document he asserted that: "If I were nominated for the presidency by any body of my fellow citizens, designated by any name they might choose to adopt, I should esteem it an honor, and would accept such nomination provided it had been made entirely independent of party consideration."[24] In the later widely published letter to Captain J. S. Allison, his brother-in-law, Taylor declared his allegiance to the Whig cause, but attempted to maintain a detached attitude which would be attractive to Democrats. Thereafter his strength grew until his nomination at the Whig National Convention in June.

In Florida both Whigs and Democrats held their nominating conventions in April, 1848. The Democrats, meeting at Madison, chose for governor William Bailey, the Jefferson County planter whom the Whigs had approached in 1845. Old William P. DuVal, former territorial governor, former Conservative party member, and once a supporter of William Henry Harrison, was nominated for Congress. For presidential electors the Democratic convention designated John Milton, Jackson County planter, George R. Fairbanks, St. Augustine lawyer and civic leader, and Charles H. Dupont, Gadsden County lawyer-planter and a former member of the Conservative party. In 1848, it seems, sensing the tide against them, Florida Democrats tried to select candidates that would be pleasing to the Whigs.[25]

The Marianna *Whig* light-heartedly noted that having tried to

23. Marianna *Florida Whig*, October 27, 1847, March 8, 1848; Tallahassee *Florida Sentinel*, February 8, 1848.

24. Zachary Taylor to Peter Sken Smith, January 30, 1848, in Marianna *Florida Whig*, March 15, 1848.

25. Marianna *Florida Whig*, April 5, 1848.

defeat Congressman Cabell with out-and-out Democrats, the Democratic party had been reduced to the adoption of a "heathen deity" as its patron saint. When in accepting the Congressional nomination, DuVal cited his past record as "the best guarantee I can offer for my future action," the *Whig* commented: "Ex-Governor DuVal is known to be a most inveterate joker."[26] The *Sentinel* took equal delight in attacking DuVal's past course and ridiculing his defense.

Unlike the Democrats, the Whigs held no central convention, but staged county meetings, each of which chose delegates to one of three divisional conventions. Each divisional convention named one presidential elector and large delegations to the Whig National Convention. Some years earlier the neutral *Star* had observed of the Whig party that it "operated without permitting the hand which impelled the movement to be seen. And it therefore had the means of combining influences and elements of power, which were also unseen, and unappreciated."[27] That there was such unseen collaboration in 1848 is apparent in the ease with which the three conventions named the same candidates. One convention made the nominations which were then endorsed by the other two and referred back to the original county meetings for ratification. In this manner the Whigs maintained the illusion of popular participation which, they maintained, the Democratic conventions prevented.

The West Florida Whig convention renominated Representative Cabell and selected for the governorship Thomas Brown. Brown was a former member of both the Nucleus and the Conservative party and had been intimately associated with the Union Bank. A Tallahassee hotel man and former planter, he had also seen service in both the territorial and state legislatures. As Zachary Taylor was dubbed "Old Rough and Ready," so the Florida papers affectionately stamped Brown "Old Matter of Fact." The West Florida convention also named Jackson Morton of Pensacola as presidential elector, with A. G. Semmes, a former Bank of Pensacola official, as alternate.[28] The Middle Florida convention endorsed the West Florida nominations and added to the list Samuel Spencer as its presidential elector, with George W. Call, Jr., brother of Wilkinson Call, as alternate. In East Florida the slate was endorsed and John H. McIntosh, a Duval County planter, was named as elector.

26. April 12, May 3, 1848.   27. October 17, 1845.
28. Marianna *Florida Whig,* May 3, 1848.

26

At the state level the bitterest race was that between DuVal and Cabell. DuVal was alternately pictured by the Whigs as a joker and as a scheming self-seeker. One widely circulated charge against DuVal was that he was the father of the ill-fated Florida banks. During his governorship he had vetoed the charters of several banks, insisting that he could approve an institution only if it were truly "the Planter's bank." This fact was made the basis of the charges in 1848 that he was solely responsible for the establishment of the banks and the "faith bonds" in Florida. This was bulwarked by the fact that as a member of Congress from Kentucky he had cast a vote three times in favor of the Bank of the United States. The *Sentinel* concluded that "if connection with the Bank is a crime, which the democracy affirms, then are the skirts of William P. DuVal black, reeking and clotted with guilt."[29]

At its convention (June, 1848) in Philadelphia the Whig party named Taylor as its presidential candidate, with Millard Fillmore, an old-line Whig, as its nominee for vice-president. Taylor's convention victory was due to a coalition of proslavery Whigs and Northern Whig leaders who realized the popularity of Taylor with the masses of people. The alliance was facilitated by Thurlow Weed of New York.[30] Though many of them had favored Clay, the Florida Whigs now closed ranks behind Taylor and Fillmore.

Meanwhile the Democratic National Convention, meeting at Baltimore in May, had nominated Senator Lewis Cass of Michigan and William O. Butler of Kentucky as their presidential and vice-presidential candidates, respectively. Cass was feared by many Southerners as an advocate of popular sovereignty, and in the North he was disliked because he favored the annexation of Texas and opposed the Wilmot Proviso.[31] Florida Democratic nominees for presidential electors had been instructed by their state convention to oppose any candidate who favored popular sovereignty, and the action of the national convention left Florida Democrats in an awkward position, to the unmixed delight of the busy Whigs. While the *Florida Whig* waited to see if Democrats would "sacrifice upon the altar of party loyalty the dearest rights of the South," the Demo-

29. Quoted *ibid.,* August 5, 1848; see also August 19, 1848.
30. Binkley, p. 178.
31. Allan Nevins, *Ordeal of the Union* (2 vols., New York, 1947), I, 192-193.

cratic State Executive Committee decided to back the action of the national convention. This not only pleased the Whigs, but divided the Democrats. Benjamin F. Whitner, the chairman of the committee, resigned in protest and was replaced by John P. DuVal. The Democratic Jacksonville *News* bitterly assailed the action of the committee, asserting: "As East Florida has to do all the voting, she is determined not to enter blindfold into a Presidential contest to gratify the whim of a few wire pullers in Tallahassee."[32]

The campaigning in Florida was hot and heavy during the summer and fall. Brown made a few speeches in which he impressed his listeners with his gentleness and kindness of heart, but the real burden was carried by the Congressional candidates. In addition to the record of DuVal, the major issue was the relative merits of the national candidates and parties in regard to slavery. Many Whigs believed that the Democrats had exhibited a "lust for conquest and annexation" which endangered the Union, drained the treasury, and sapped the energies of the country.[33]

As if circumstances were not already favorable enough to the Whigs, a convention of Northern antislavery forces met at Buffalo, New York, in August to form the Free Soil party. There the old Jacksonian Democrat, Martin Van Buren, was named the party candidate for president, with Charles Francis Adams for vice-president.[34] The effect of this action was that more voters were attracted by the Free Soilers from the Democrats than from the Whigs. Before the summer was over, the election of Taylor seemed certain, and in Florida a Whig triumph seemed likely. Retaining its most distinguished Northern leadership, and being rid of some of its anti-slavery element, the Whig party was represented as being the great middle-of-the-road national party which would preserve the Union.

The state elections were held in October, while the presidential election took place in November. In the Congressional race Cabell defeated DuVal by 577 votes, 4,382 to 3,805. Thomas Brown won the governorship from William Bailey, 4,145 to 3,646. In both houses of the General Assembly the Whigs retained control and again organized those houses.[35] Erasmus D. Tracey of Nassau

32. Quoted in Marianna *Florida Whig*, July 1, 1848.
33. *Ibid.*, February 16, July 15, 1848.   34. Nevins, I, 206-207.
35. Marianna *Florida Whig*, December 2, 1848.

County became president of the senate, and Benjamin Putnam of St. Johns County became speaker of the house. Charles W. Downing was held over as secretary of the senate, while William B. Lancaster became secretary of the house.[36] All four were East Florida men, probably to compensate for the fact that the governor and representative were from Middle Florida.

Despite the increased majority for Cabell and the victory for Brown, the Whigs added only three small counties to the list which Cabell had carried in the mid-term election of 1846. In that year Cabell had carried Escambia, Santa Rosa, Walton, and Jackson counties in West Florida, Gadsden, Leon, Wakulla, and Madison counties in Middle Florida, and only Nassau and Duval counties in East Florida.[37] All of these except Escambia, Duval, and Nassau had favored statehood in 1839. Generally speaking, the counties which had opposed statehood became Democratic counties. These Democratic counties were also usually the ones with the least population, the least valuable farm land, the fewest slaves, and the smallest cotton production.[38]

In 1848 Hamilton and Calhoun counties were added to the Whig list by the closest of margins, and Levy County was overwhelmingly carried by the party. Cabell carried Columbia County by five votes, while Brown lost it by twenty-one. In the November presidential election Taylor carried all the counties which Cabell had won and added to them Alachua and Marion counties in East Florida and Washington County in West Florida. The vote for the Whig electors was 4,539 to 3,238.[39] The large vote in the presidential and congressional races would seem to indicate that the Florida voter was showing greater interest in the national political issues than in those primarily of local significance.

36. *Niles' Weekly Register,* December 13, 1848.
37. Tallahassee *Floridian,* November 21, 1846.
38. *Ibid.,* September 28, 1839; see also *Seventh Census of the United States: 1850* (Washington, 1853), pp 400-401, 407-408.
39. Marianna *Florida Whig,* December 2, 1848; *Niles' Weekly Register,* January 10, 1849.

3. YEARS OF CRISIS

In 1849 and 1850 the Whig party in Florida reached the height of its power and influence. Its leadership might be characterized as "safe and sane," promoting programs of conservatism and moderation, while the Whig newspapers were particularly capable and well managed. In West Florida the Marianna *Florida Whig* was published by Thomas B. Alexander and had come to be the leading Whig voice of that section. In Pensacola the *Gazette* was still functioning as a pro-Whig paper, but since the retirement of Benjamin D. Wright from the editorship in 1846, it had come to be viewed as less authoritative than before. In Tallahassee the *Florida Sentinel* under the skilled hand of Joseph Clisby was maintaining its position as the leading Middle Florida organ. Because of its location in the capital, its prestige as an older paper, and its moderate tone, it was undoubtedly the most influential Whig paper in the state and was widely quoted by the other state papers.

In East Florida, where the Whigs had been weakest, determined efforts had been made to strengthen the newspaper representation of the party. After the Democrats bought out the St. Augustine *News*, its former editor, Thomas T. Russell, briefly edited the *Florida Whig and People's Advocate* at Jacksonville.[1] In Palatka the *Whig Banner* was published for a short time by George M. Grouard.[2] Neither of these were important papers, however, and Congressman Cabell took steps to establish a well supported, influential publication. With the assistance of Samuel L. Burritt, a Whig lawyer and member of the state senate from Duval County, he induced Columbus Drew to come to Florida in 1848 and to commence the publication of the *Florida Republican* at Jacksonville.[3] Young Drew, a Virginian born of English parents, had worked for the *National Intelligencer* in Washington. Conservative in outlook and attached to the Union, he proved an influential addition to the ranks of Florida Whiggery, and under his hand the *Republican*

1. St. Augustine *Florida Herald,* May 6, 1845.
2. James Owen Knauss, *Territorial Florida Journalism* (DeLand, 1926), p. 66.
3. Alice J. Drew, *Columbus Drew, Something of His Life and Ancestry* (Jacksonville, 1910), pp. 93-95.

was soon ranked as one of the leading Whig journals of the South. In addition to the four larger papers, smaller sheets of less influence and permanency supported the Whigs in 1848. In Gadsden County C. J. Bartlett's *Quincy Times* backed the Whigs, while on the Gulf Coast the Apalachicola *Commercial Advertiser* under R. J. Young and R. A. Dominge upheld the cause, and in frontier Ocala the *Argus* helped bolster Eastern Whiggery.[4]

In the October, 1848, election the Whigs renewed their control of the General Assembly. This session of the Assembly was responsible for electing a United States Senator to fill the seat of James D. Westcott, whose term would expire in March, 1849. It was a foregone conclusion that Democrat Westcott would not be returned. The *Pensacola Gazette* and the Marianna *Florida Whig* reflected the desire of Whigs in their section for the selection of a man from the "neglected" West. The *Whig* advanced Jesse J. Finley, a Jackson County lawyer, while Pensacola interests pushed Jackson Morton, a prominent businessman of that city.[5] Rumors were afloat that Cabell was intriguing for the office, but he does not seem to have been interested in it.[6]

On December 11, 1848, a joint meeting of the two houses of the General Assembly was held to choose the new United States Senator. On the first ballot Morton and Finley were nominated, as were George T. Ward of Tallahassee and Samuel L. Burritt of Jacksonville. All were Whigs. Burritt led but did not receive the required majority on the five ballots which were cast on that day. His support came overwhelmingly from Democrats and a scattering of East Florida Whigs. Finley's backers, seven in number, were with one exception Whigs and were from Middle Florida and West Florida. The support for Ward was almost exclusively from Middle Florida Whigs; no Democrats supported him and only three East Florida Whigs. After the third ballot John Ghent, an independent, nominated a Pensacola Democrat, Walker Anderson, but this maneuver did not draw away most of the Democrats supporting Burritt.[7]

4. *Quincy Times,* May 13, 1848; *Ocala Argus,* June 8, 1848; Knauss, p. 34.   5. Marianna *Florida Whig,* November 25, 1848.
6. Jacksonville *News,* October 8, 1847.
7. Tallahassee *Florida Sentinel,* December 12, 1848; Florida *Senate Journal* (1848), pp. 48-50; Florida *House Journal* (1848), pp. 47-49.

This contest evidenced the strong sectionalism still remaining among the Whigs and the laxity of their party discipline. The jealousy of the Middle Florida group which existed among Easterners and Westerners burst into the open. Both the Pensacola and Jacksonville Whig papers were critical of the tendency of the Middle Florida Whigs to make off with the lion's share of the spoils. "The West is *entitled* to the appointment," wrote the *Pensacola Gazette,* "and *we insist upon our claim."*[8] The *Florida Republican* in Jacksonville explained: "So far as a sectional claim is worth considering, we denied any whatever to Middle Florida, conceded the first to the West, and only preferred that of the East as 'next in point of validity.' "[9]

After the unsuccessful balloting ended on December 11, no further attempt to elect a senator could be arranged until January 1, 1849. On that date only Ward and Morton were nominated, and Morton was chosen on the second ballot by a vote of 30-27. An alliance of the Democrats and Whigs who had supported Burritt and those who had earlier supported Morton had been effected, so that Florida's first Whig Senator was elected by twenty-two Democrats and eight Whigs. The Whigs were Owen Avery and William N. Richburg of Escambia, Charles A. Tweed and John Wilkinson of Santa Rosa, Samuel Burritt and James W. Bryant of Duval, William P. Moseley of Madison, and David S. Walker of Leon.[10] Democrats had been happy to defeat Ward, an old staunch champion of Whig principles, by backing the less able Morton. It seems likely that other considerations were connected, involving vote-swapping on the chartering of railroads and the election of other officers, but the evidence is slim and circumstantial.

The most important of the other offices which it fell to the lot of the General Assembly to elect were the heads of the state executive departments. All those chosen were Whigs, and in every case there was no important contest. Charles W. Downing was named secretary of state; David Hogue, attorney general; Simon Towle, comptroller; and William R. Hayward, treasurer. All were from Middle Florida.[11]

8. Quoted in Tallahassee *Floridian,* December 9, 1848.
9. January 18, 1849; see also December 21, 1848.
10. Florida *Senate Journal* (1848), pp. 144-145; Florida *House Journal* (1848), p. 127.
11. Tallahassee *Florida Sentinel,* January 9, 1849.

In addition to the election of the executive officers for which the General Assembly normally was responsible, Governor-elect Thomas Brown soon confronted the body with a dilemma concerning his own assumption of office. Governor Moseley had been elected on May 26, 1845, according to proclamations for such election by the last territorial governor and the surviving members of the Committee of the Constitutional Convention of 1838. The constitution specified that the first officers of the state, no matter when elected, should serve for four years from the first Monday in October. To complicate matters, the proclamation of the Committee of the Constitutional Convention had specified that the governor should serve four years beginning May 26, 1845. Brown contended that under the constitution, Moseley should have given up office in October, 1848, since his term should be dated from the October prior to his election. Moseley contended that the office should not be occupied by Brown until October, 1849, since his term should be dated from the October after his election. The Judiciary Committee of the General Assembly in 1845 had made a report upholding the 1849 date for which Moseley contended. Then Brown asked the legislature in January, 1849, to resolve the issue.[12]

Differences of opinion marked the views of the legislators, and many felt that a decision on the tenure of an office created by the constitution was beyond the power of the General Assembly. There was general agreement, with but few exceptions, that the governor must take the oath of office in the presence of the Assembly, even though Moseley had not done so. Ultimately the decision of the legislature was to hold the inauguration on Saturday, January 13, at ten in the evening, but no decision was reached as to when Brown's term should begin. By the simple expedient of not getting out, Moseley remained in office until October of 1849, and Brown did not further contest the issue.[13]

On January 13 at the appointed hour Brown was escorted to the speaker's stand in the Hall of Representatives and charged by Representative David S. Walker to ever act as a sentinel for the state. After the oath was administered by Chief Justice Thomas Douglas, Brown delivered his inaugural address. He expressed grave

---

12. Thomas Brown to the Senate and the House of Representatives of the Florida General Assembly, Tallahassee *Florida Sentinel*, January 9, 1849.
13. Jacksonville *Florida Republican*, February 1, 1849.

concern over the national controversies centering around slavery and pledged his adherence to the sovereignty of the states, the rights of the South, and the compromises of the Constitution. He startled and angered many who heard and read his words, however, when he cautioned that there was a vast difference between manly resistance to unjust encroachment "and the empty vapouring and gasconade which has become so common." He condemned the "intrigues of partisan politicians" which had made disunion and dissolution household words. "I believe," he warned, "that the Northern fanatics have done much to weaken the attachment and reverence of the people for the Union; and I fear as much has been done by Southern demagogues as Northern fanatics."[14]

After the adjournment of the General Assembly, both Whig and Democratic papers found some things to praise in its record. Most universally approved was an act establishing a common school system to be supported by local taxation and the proceeds of the sale of public lands given to the state by the federal government. The state register of public lands was to be ex-officio the state superintendent of schools, and the judges of probate were to be the county superintendents. In each county school districts were to be administered by three trustees popularly elected. They were to levy local school taxes.[15] At the same session the legislature also made the offices of register of public lands and judges of probate elective by the people. Unfortunately, since public opinion did not endorse public education at public expense, these two moves seem to have cancelled each other and little or nothing was done to establish schools. Other than these acts, the most generally approved bills were three railroad acts, though there was much doubt that two of the roads would be constructed.[16] The road which did get under way was the Atlantic and Gulf Railroad, which soon came under the control of David Yulee.

The Assembly also passed resolutions decrying sectional strife and all Northern actions which were marked by unkindness, wrong, insult, and injury. They asserted that there was no party division in the South on questions involving Southern rights and the institu-

14. Tallahassee *Florida Sentinel,* January 16, 1849.
15. Tallahassee *Floridian,* January 20, 1849.
16. *Ibid.,* January 13, 1849; Tallahassee *Florida Sentinel,* January 16, 1849.

tion of slavery, and they declared the willingness of Florida to join with other Southern states in defense of their rights "by whatever means the highest wisdom of all shall suggest."[17]

Concern for the rights of the South was growing among the people of the state, though it was most vociferously expressed by the radical wing of the Democratic party. Cabell had not joined in Calhoun's "Southern Address" earlier, and he was taunted with this fact in 1849. In Madison County a public meeting adopted resolutions critical of Cabell, and a similar meeting was reported in Gadsden County. A protest meeting in Jacksonville met with less popular response, causing the *Republican* to conclude: "There is not that excitement among the *people* which we are sometimes led to believe exists."[18] Many Whigs, however, approved Cabell's course, feeling that the best way to protect Southern interests was by cooperation between conservative, propertied interests North and South. Slavery was a troublesome issue to them, if agitated in an emotional way on a sectional basis, and was seen as dangerous to the Union as well as to their interests. The attitude of these Whigs was expressed by the *Florida Republican* when it declared that nine-tenths of the Southern people would "stand up for the rights of the South. Every true Southern representative will not fail to give his vote and lift his voice in opposition to the schemes of northern incendiaries; but few will be found rash enough to propose disunion for a remedy. It is no remedy. It will kill, not cure, the patient."[19]

The criticism at home of his action was not lost on Representative Cabell, however. When the Whig caucus met in December, 1849, to organize the House of Representatives of the Thirty-first Congress, Southern members tried to commit the party to oppose exclusion of slavery from the territories and its abolition in the District of Columbia. On the defeat of this attempt, eight Southern Whigs, including Cabell, withdrew from the caucus and refused to aid in the organization of the House. The minority Democrats subsequently elected Howell Cobb of Georgia to the Speakership. Cabell defended his act as a blow for the rights of the South and characterized those who were critical of him as Northern men or timid and unworthy Southern men. He declared his belief that

17. Jacksonville *Florida Republican,* February 1, 1849.
18. March 15, 1849; Tallahassee *Florida Sentinel,* February 20, 1849.
19. June 14, 1849.

Southern institutions and the Union were in real peril from the antislavery agitation.[20]

During 1849 feeling in the South, particularly among the Democratic followers of Calhoun, in favor of a convention of Southern states to devise means for mutual protection had been growing. This sentiment had been fanned by continued attempts in Congress to enact the principles of the Wilmot Proviso, by efforts to bring California into the Union as a free state, thus upsetting the sectional balance of power, and by resolutions of Northern state legislatures who ultimately all, except that of Iowa, asserted the duty of Congress to prohibit slavery in all the territories. A number of legislatures called for the abolition of slavery and of the slave trade in the District of Columbia.[21]

Late in 1849 Senator Yulee suggested to Calhoun a meeting of the governors of Southern states or the formation of a Southern political party to offset the power of the Northern antislavery forces.[22] Calhoun evidently had been considering some such course, and he succeeded in manipulating the call for a general convention of Southern states through an invitation issued by a state convention in Mississippi. The proposed Southern Convention was to be held at Nashville in June of 1850.[23] News of the proposal was met in Florida with mixed reactions from the Whig press. The Jacksonville *Republican* saw no harm in the mutual consultation of the slave states, but the Tallahassee *Sentinel* feared that more harm than good might result. The latter paper noted the ill feeling pervading the halls of Congress and asserted: "It is mortifying to see a temper pervading the national councils which would disgrace a village debating society, and we are sorry to see the press and letter writers fanning, instead of throwing water upon the flame."[24]

As the people debated the Nashville Convention, Governor Brown remained silent and took no action to endorse the meeting or to name delegates to it. Some intimation of his attitude might have

20. Jacksonville *Florida Republican,* December 13, 1849, February 7, 1850; James Bulger Mool, "Florida in Federal Politics" (Master's thesis, Duke University, 1940), p. 50.

21. Allan Nevins, *Ordeal of the Union* (2 Vols., New York, 1947), I, 255.

22. Mills M. Lord, Jr., "David Levy Yulee, Statesman and Railroad Builder" (Master's thesis, University of Florida, 1940), p. 73.

23. Jacksonville *Florida Republican,* January 10, 1850.

24. *Ibid.;* Tallahassee *Florida Sentinel,* January 14, 29, 1850.

been gathered, however, from the fact that the Whig newspapers took an increasingly hostile view of the meeting, intimating that its movers had disunion in mind.

Meanwhile, in Washington on January 29, 1850, Senator Henry Clay of Kentucky presented to the United States Senate a series of compromise resolutions which were to effect "an amicable arrangement of all questions in controversy between the free and slave states, growing out of the subject of slavery."[25] Clay had returned to the Senate from a seven-year retirement determined to engineer another great compromise which might save the Union. The resolutions which he introduced would admit California with no mention of slavery, set up territorial governments in the rest of the Mexican cession with no restrictions upon slavery, indemnify Texas for giving up her claims to New Mexico, abolish the slave trade in the District of Columbia, prevent the abolition of slavery in the federal district without the consent of Maryland and the compensation of slaveholders, provide a more stringent fugitive slave law, and record the inability of Congress to hinder the slave trade between slave states.[26]

All over the nation extremists on both sides of the question assailed the measures. In Florida the Democratic papers were critical. The St. Augustine *Ancient City* dubbed the measures the "surrender bill." The Whig Jacksonville *Republican* was disappointed that nothing more "original" had come from the great statesman, but noted that this might reflect the tremendous complexity of the problem.[27] Generally the Whig papers were favorable to the compromise measures and highly critical of the attacks made upon them in Congress by Calhoun and his followers. Though the Whigs did not always question the South Carolinian's sincerity, they probably agreed with the *Florida Republican* that "an idiosyncrasy possesses him, which nothing can exorcise, but the clang of arms, and the din of conflict over the fragments of a broken Union."[28] This paper deftly pointed out that Calhoun's batteries were directed less against the North than against "our system of government," and the editor lamented that Calhoun would destroy the glory of "the most colossal power on the globe."

25. Jacksonville *Florida Republican*, February 14, 1850.
26. Nevins, I, 233; John B. McMaster, *A History of the People of the United States* (8 vols., New York, 1883-1913) VIII, 12-13.
27. February 14, 1850.   28. April 11, 1850.

Ten days after Clay introduced his compromise measures, the entire Florida Congressional delegation, Yulee, Morton, and Cabell, sent a joint letter to Governor Brown calling upon him to endorse the Nashville Convention and to arrange for Florida's representation in it. They declared that "timely preventives" must be employed to prevent the federal government from becoming an instrument of ultimate ruin for the South. They saw united action by the people of the South as the only effective check on this tendency. Organized resistance, wisely directed, would arrest aggressions on Southern rights.[29]

Cabell, who had previously opposed a Southern convention, sent a separate letter to Brown explaining his position. He related that he had joined in the message because the Nashville meeting was to be only an advisory session to "define the position of the South" and to propose methods of redress in certain contingencies. "We wish to prevent the passage of laws which we are pledged to resist," he wrote, "or, if we cannot prevent aggression and outrage, we should be prepared to resist."[30] Cabell had little hope for compromise at this point and feared that the antislavery forces would triumph for he told Brown: "I shall stay at my post, and resist, by all lawful means, the consummation of measures hostile to the interest of my state. . . . But as the sentiment of Congress is against us, and as measures of compromise can only be carried by the influence of men who are candidates for the Presidency . . . I have little hope that my resistance will be availing."[31]

Brown's reply to the joint letter of the Congressional delegation was a repudiation of sectional measures, and it warmed the hearts of all Union men. He flatly declared: "I consider such a convention as revolutionary in its tendency, and directly against the spirit if not the letter of the Constitution of the United States."[32] He regretted that he had been asked to take part in the movement, saying that he had hoped the people could judge it without his involvement, and he declined to appoint delegates to Nashville on the grounds that he had no authority to take such action. He believed that there was nothing the convention could do save constitute itself a

29. David Yulee, Jackson Morton, and Edward Cabell to Thomas Brown, February 6, 1850, in Jacksonville *Florida Republican*, March 7, 1850.
30. Cabell to Brown, February 12, 1850, *ibid*.   31. *Ibid*
32. Brown to Yulee, Morton, and Cabell, February 22, 1850, *ibid*.

revolutionary body. If that should be the purpose, he wrote, "I most solemnly protest against it. The time has not arrived for such measures, and I pray God such a time may never arrive."

Brown observed that in the entire question of relations between North and South, "Time has brought forth no wisdom—experience has brought no knowledge. The Northern *politician,* gaining confidence in this wordy conflict assumes a more *threatening* tone, and the Southern *politician,* to keep even pace, must become more violent in his manner of resistance, and *threaten still louder.* . . . And still I believe that this glorious Union will firmly and safely weather this storm."[33]

The Whig press in Florida approved Brown's course, while the Democratic press almost as unanimously opposed it. The *Republican* spoke darkly of a few "Brutuses" who wished to destroy the Union at Nashville, while the *Floridian* denounced those who "yielded" to the view of Governor Brown.[34] The *Florida Whig* reported that the people of West Florida were not interested in the convention and were as calm as if the legislators at Washington were attending to the legitimate business of legislation rather than crying "to arms." The *Commercial Advertiser* viewed the attitude of Whigs as conciliatory but firm, while that of Democrats was harsh and abusive, and it concluded: "The spirit of the Whig is decidedly better to operate on the great conservative mind and heart of the North." The *Pensacola Gazette* was amazed that Senator Morton had endorsed the Convention, and the newspaper ranked Brown's slashing retort with Jackson's squelching of nullification in 1832.[35]

Though he was a Whig, Morton's views on the sectional disputes did not coincide with those held by most of the Whig hierarchy in Florida. Rather they seemed almost to be a carbon copy of the views of his abler senatorial colleague Yulee. Morton slapped back at Brown as representing neither of the parties in Florida and as giving aid and comfort to the adversaries of the South. The Nashville Convention, he asserted, was designed to save the Union if that were possible, or to save the South if it were not. He asked what it would take to make Brown calculate the value of the Union and declared: "The Nashville Convention will, I presume, suggest such means and measures as may be advisable for the South to adopt to

33. *Ibid.*   34. *Ibid.,* March 7, 21, 1850.
35. All quoted *ibid.,* April 11, 1850.

preserve her liberty and independence. Call this 'revolutionary,' if you choose, and 'make the most of it.' "[36]

Brown's reply, couched in terms of condescension, expressed regret that Morton had not more experience in public affairs and commented that when he had acquired it he would regret his action. Brown remarked of himself that he had been born at the close of the American Revolution, and asserted: "I do not wish to see another revolution, and if I feel called upon to blush in this connection, it is for those who pronounce this government a Russian despotism —who would call a convention of modern politicians to remedy the inherent defects in the great Charter of our liberties—who think themselves able to improve it—who in respect to anticipated grievances would change or destroy it—and who seek to delude the people with dazzling schemes of a Southern Confederacy."[37]

Despite the opposition of Whig leaders to the Nashville Convention, its popular appeal was apparently greater than the Whig press had been willing to admit at first. By April the *Florida Republican* was forced to concede that the Convention and the stand of the Florida Congressional delegation were not unsupported, but it insisted that support was not as unanimous as the Democrats made out.[38] Gradually the Whigs began to agree that since the Convention could not be prevented, it might be best to send moderate men to control it. Brown's refusal to appoint delegates to Nashville was circumvented by supporters of the movement through bipartisan courthouse meetings which selected delegates to district meetings in East, West, and Middle Florida, which meetings in turn named delegates to Nashville. At Ocala the East Florida meeting chose Joseph M. Hernandez, Whig, and B. M. Pearson, Democrat, as delegates. At Tallahassee the Middle Florida meeting named Charles H. Dupont, Democrat, and Arthur J. Forman, Whig, as delegates, with R. W. Williams, Whig, and Augustus E. Maxwell, Democrat, as alternates. The West Florida meeting at Marianna selected Cabell and James F. McClellan, a Democrat, as delegates. Hernandez and Cabell did not attend the Convention.[39]

Meanwhile in Congress disunion sentiment had rapidly subsided

36. Morton to Brown, March 10, 1850, *ibid.*, April 4, 1850.
37. Brown to Morton, March 30, 1850, *ibid.*, April 11, 1850.
38. March 21, April 4, 25, 1850.
39. Jacksonville *Florida Republican*, May 9, 23, 1850.

in March and April. On the seventh of March Daniel Webster had delivered a bold oration upholding Clay's compromise, denouncing secessionists and abolitionists alike, and calling for the preservation of the Union.[40] Florida Whigs hailed the speech as a harbinger of hope, and Cabell hailed both Clay and Webster as "bearing themselves nobly toward the country."[41] Stephen A. Douglas of Illinois and his friends busied themselves in the interests of a compromise settlement. And on March 31 John C. Calhoun, the genius of the radical Southern Democrats, died.

In an atmosphere of growing conciliation the Nashville Convention assembled on June 3 with Alabama, Arkansas, Florida, Georgia, Mississippi, South Carolina, Tennessee, Texas, and Virginia represented, though some delegates had very dubious authority to speak for their people. William L. Sharkey, a Mississippi conservative, was elected president, and the whole tone of the meeting was far more moderate than had been anticipated. Though the principal resolution of the meeting expressed a willingness to see the western territories divided between the sections by extending the Missouri Compromise line, the South Carolinians managed to get a resolution passed condemning the Clay compromise measures. After the passage of resolutions, however, conservative counsel prevailed, and the Convention adjourned to await the action of Congress on the Compromise.[42]

Despite the growing sentiment for a settlement on conciliatory lines, the Florida Democratic press continued to rail at "submission" to the Compromise. All Democrats did not take the line which their press did, however, and one member of a Democratic state convention publicly declared that the Tallahassee *Floridian* totally misrepresented the views of the Florida Democracy. He declared that the Whig *Sentinel* represented Democratic views on the Compromise far better than did the Democratic papers. The editor of the *Sentinel* asserted that he had talked to no one, Whig or Democrat, who was against the Compromise.[43]

Meanwhile the backers of the Compromise in Congress had been fighting a long, bitter, uphill fight against the Southern extremists,

40. Nevins, I, 288-291, 315.
41. Jacksonville *Florida Republican,* March 21, April 25, 1850.
42. *Ibid.,* June 13, 27, 1850; Nevins, I, 315-317.
43. St. Augustine *Ancient City,* June 22, 1850; Tallahassee *Florida Sentinel,* July 9, 1850.

the Northern free-soil forces, and the administration of President Taylor. Influenced by pride, jealousy, obstinacy, and hatred for Clay, Taylor had thrown the full weight of his influence against the Compromise. Calhoun's death on the last day of March, however, was followed by Taylor's death on July 9. Not only were the forces of opposition weakened by these events, but the forces of compromise were strengthened, for the new President, Millard Fillmore, threw the influence of his administration behind the Clay measures.[44]

By mid-August a series of bills embodying the principal features of the Compromise had been enacted. California was to be admitted as a free state, in the rest of the Mexican cession territorial governments were to be established with no reference to slavery restrictions, the slave trade in the District of Columbia was abolished, Texas was compensated for giving up her claims to New Mexico, and a stringent fugitive slave law was approved. The entire Florida delegation opposed the California and slave-trade bills and favored the organization of the territories.[45] Cabell favored the indemnification of Texas, while Morton and Yulee opposed it.[46] All three are believed to have favored the fugitive slave law, though Cabell registered no vote on it in the house and there was no roll call on the final vote in the Senate.[47] Cabell was the only one of the group to support the Compromise as a whole after its passage.

In the Congressional election of 1850 in Florida all other issues were subordinated to that of the Compromise. The Democrats vigorously attacked it, while the Whigs as warmly defended it. In convention at Suwannee Springs, the Democrats named John Beard for Congress and for the first time adopted no platform. Beard's most outstanding public service to this time had been as register of public lands. The Whigs tore into Beard and his party with telling sarcasm. Beard was found to have been an ardent supporter of Harrison in 1840 and was charged with having accepted office at the hands of Whig President Tyler.[48] The failure of the Democrats to write a platform was charged to the fact that the Nashville Convention had been meeting and the Compromise was still being

44. Nevins, I, 318-319, 337.
45. *Congressional Globe,* 31 Congress, 1 Session, pp. 1573, 1589, 1772, 1776, 1830, 1837.
46. *Ibid.,* pp. 1555, 1764.   47. *Ibid.,* pp. 1647, 1660, 1807.
48. Jacksonville *Florida Republican,* July 25, 1850.

debated in Congress at the time their convention met. Democrats, said the Whigs, had not known what to favor and what to oppose.[49]

By general consent Cabell was to be the Whig standard-bearer in Florida again. County meetings were held to endorse his candidacy and to adopt resolutions favoring the Compromise. Since there was no state convention, there was no formal Whig platform, but the resolutions of the county meetings, the professions of Cabell, and the editorials of the Whig press soon made the Compromise and preservation of the Union the Whig campaign principles.[50]

Beard, in his campaign, formulated the stand which came to be associated with the Democrats. It was simply opposition to the Compromise. "I love the Union with a *reasonable affection*," wrote Beard, "not with a servile or superstitious reverence, as some great invisible deity." He could see nothing that the South had gained in the Compromise and proclaimed: "For one I will never agree to any such terms; they may call me *traitor*, disunionist, or what they please; I would resist to the 'last extremity.' "[51] This was the theme Beard preached all over Florida.

Cabell accepted the gauntlet thrown by Beard and faced him squarely on the issue. "Major Beard is for 'a dissolution of the Union' because of the passage of the . . . bills, which together make up the 'Omnibus' or 'Compromise Bill.' I am not. The issues are Union or disunion—I am for Union: Peace or war—I am for peace."[52] The Whigs also appealed to the old Jacksonian Democrats, recounted Jackson's opposition to nullification, and told the "old-fashioned Democrats" that their party now denounced their hero's doctrines as federalism. Though Beard continued to attack the Compromise and to attempt to brand it as a creature of the abolitionists, Cabell stood firm in his stand that it was a measure to keep the peace, to save the Union. "Never," he declared, "either as Representative or Candidate, will I assume the awful responsibility of recommending to you a dissolution of the Union."[53]

Beard was not opposed on the stump personally by Cabell, who was in Washington all during the campaign, but the Whig cause was ably sustained by David S. Walker. Speaking often in conjunction with Richard K. Call or George T. Ward, he campaigned for the

49. Tallahassee *Florida Sentinel*, July 2, 1850.   50. *Ibid.*, August 13, 1850.
51. Jacksonville *Florida Republican*, September 26, 1850.
52. *Ibid.*   53. Tallahassee *Florida Sentinel*, September 17, 24, 1850.

re-election of Cabell and for his own election to the post of register of public lands. Opposing Walker for this post was the Democrat Mariano D. Papy. Papy expressly disclaimed the dissolution doctrines propounded by his fellow Democrat Beard, and advocated division of the western territories by an extension of the Missouri Compromise line.[54] The Whig newspapers followed the line laid down by Cabell and Walker, the *Sentinel* declaring that the election would show whether or not the people of Florida stood on the platform of the "revolutionists." The *Republican* urged, "Let us unite in the State, and elect the Upholder of the South and Defender of the Union, E. C. Cabell."[55]

In the October election Cabell and Walker were victorious, and one Whig editor proclaimed that their triumph was proof that "the people have declared for Compromise—have chosen peace—have spoken in thunder tones for Union—and demanded adherence to 'non-intervention.' "[56] The overall election results, however, show that the Democrats had gained from the controversies of the previous two years. Cabell's majority was smaller than in 1848, and the Whigs lost control of the General Assembly, although the Democratic majority in the senate was only one and in the house of representatives, two. Cabell's 1848 majority of 577 had dropped to 481 as he defeated Beard 4,531 to 4,050. Though fewer votes were cast in the race for register of public lands, Walker's majority was 629 as he defeated Papy 4,414 to 3,785. Though he had run on virtually the same issues as Cabell, Walker had not been involved in the Nashville Convention controversy, nor had the lines been as sharply drawn between him and his opponent as they had been between Cabell and Beard.[57]

Cabell carried most of the more populous counties in the state, which were also usually those having the most valuable farm land, producing the most cotton and tobacco, and paying the greatest amount of state taxes. Beard's strength was in the large but thinly populated counties of South and East Florida and in sparsely populated Washington and Franklin counties in the West. He also carried Jefferson County, a traditionally Democratic stronghold, and

54. *Ibid.*, September 10, 1850.
55. *Ibid.*, October 1, 1850; Jacksonville *Florida Republican*, October 3, 1850.   56. Jacksonville *Florida Republican*, October 16, 1850.
57. *Pensacola Gazette*, November 9, 1850; Tallahassee *Florida Sentinel*, November 19, 1850.

the only black-belt plantation county of Middle Florida which never succumbed to the Whigs. Except for Jefferson County, those carried by Beard were the relatively poor, small farming counties.[58]

After the successful carrying of the Compromise measures and the electoral triumph of Unionists all over the South, the reconvened session of the Nashville Convention in November came as a distinct anticlimax. Few delegates attended; two of the states originally represented, Arkansas and Texas, had no representation; and the debates attracted little public attention. The extremists dominated this session, however, and it condemned most of the Compromise and called for a Southern Congress to restore the rights of the South or to provide for her safety and independence.[59]

Late in the same month, November, 1850, the fifth session of the Florida General Assembly met in Tallahassee. In this session much time was devoted to consideration of problems arising from federal-state relations. In his message to the Assembly Brown dealt with many topics, the most important touching upon education, internal improvements, banking, and the sectional controversies. Appalled by the fact that almost two-thirds of the school-age children of Florida could not read and write, he urged greater emphasis on public education. David S. Walker, who as register of public lands was ex-officio state superintendent of schools, worked diligently to promote a system of schools, but little real progress was made in this line before the Civil War.[60]

In the field of internal improvements Brown recommended to the Assembly that a board be created to control the lands granted by the federal government to the state for the financing of such improvements. This board was also to draft an overall plan for a state-wide system of improvements to eliminate what Brown termed "local disorganized projects." Following this recommendation, the Assembly created such a board to consist of one member elected by the Assembly from each judicial circuit and ex-officio members in the persons of the governor, attorney-general, treasurer, and comptroller. The elected members were James W. Bryant, Archibald T. Bennett, Richard K. Call, and John Darling.[61]

58. Tallahassee *Florida Sentinel,* February 25, 1851; *Seventh Census of the United States 1850,* pp. 400-401, 407-408.
59. Jacksonville *Florida Republican,* November 28, 1850; Nevins, I, 354.
60. Florida *Senate Journal* (1850-1851), pp. 86-87.
61. *Ibid.,* pp. 9-11; Tallahassee *Florida Sentinel,* January 28, 1851.

Brown noted that a request for a bank charter would be made of the Assembly, and he urged sympathetic consideration of the propriety of establishing a bank moderately capitalized "upon sound principles and under salutary restrictions."[62] When this application was made, the Assembly approved it and chartered the State Bank of Florida at Tallahassee. The proposed bank could not meet the high standards set for it, however, and never progressed beyond the paper stage. It is interesting to note, nonetheless, that the charter was granted by a legislature with a slight Democratic majority, a fact indicative of the almost imperceptible change taking place in the outlook of the Democrats. Not only were Whigs who feared for the rights of the South infiltrating Democratic ranks, but the Democrats themselves were losing their concern over "monied monopolies." The softening of the economic differences between the parties probably goes far to explain the generally harmonious nature of this session.[63]

In reference to sectional troubles Brown strongly urged willing and cheerful submission by all sections to the paramount law of the land. Nothing short of that, he declared, could preserve the Union "in real vitality or even in hollow semblance." Brown feared, however, that such submission might not be given, and he invited the Assembly to give him the power to call a state convention "for the purpose of devising a remedy" in the event of the repeal of the fugitive slave law or any other "aggressive" measure. He also laid before it the Nashville recommendations for a Southern Congress.

The Nashville recommendations were not acted upon by the Assembly, to the hearty approval of the *Sentinel*, which remarked that this omission should serve to "check any attempt to get up bastard representations by Court House meetings, in which not a tenth of the people are represented." Despite Brown's request for power to summon a convention, and although various other measures were before the legislature in reference to the right of secession, the absurdity of secession, fugitive slaves, and the right of revolution, no action was completed in this session on any such proposition concerning slavery.[64]

62. All references to Brown's message to the legislature are to the text published in Jacksonville *Florida Republican*, December 5, 1850, and in *Pensacola Gazette*, December 7, 1850.
63. Tallahassee *Florida Sentinel*, January 28, 1851.   64. *Ibid*.

This session of the Assembly was responsible for the election of a United States Senator to succeed Yulee in 1852. Many assumed that Yulee would automatically be re-elected by the Democratic majority, but Yulee himself had become aware of a combination against him even before the legislature had assembled. Though he received the endorsement of the Democratic caucus in December, the power of the disaffected Democrats was of serious proportions because in joint session the Democrats outnumbered the Whigs only 31-28. The hostility toward Yulee had several bases. Among Whigs, and possibly among some Democrats, opposition was based upon his radicalism on sectional issues. There was also feeling that he had neglected South Florida, which angered Democrats from Key West and from Hillsborough County. Furthermore, commercial interests which would not be served by Yulee's Fernandina to Cedar Keys railroad, chartered by the legislature of 1848-1849, wished to remove him from a position which he had utilized to shower benefits upon the road. This again involved the Key West Democrats who saw such a railroad drawing off much of their shipping traffic. Rival railroad interests in Jacksonville, St. Augustine, and Pensacola, both Whig and Democratic, were anxious to weaken Yulee. It would be difficult to say how many legislators opposed Yulee on political grounds, how many on economic grounds, or how many because of his stand on national issues—but the mixture of motives must be recognized.[65]

Thirty votes constituted the majority to elect a United States Senator, and on two ballots Yulee received twenty-nine, while the remainder were blank. On the third ballot Yulee's vote fell to twenty-eight, and on the fourth thirty-one votes were cast for Stephen Russell Mallory of Key West. Disaffected Democrats had joined with the Whigs to defeat Yulee, just as in 1849 disaffected Whigs had joined the Democrats to defeat Ward.[66] Though Yulee contested Mallory's election on the grounds that he had been elected 29-0 on the first ballot, he was unsuccessful in the contest.

Whigs were not laboring under the delusion that Mallory was their man. They made it plain that neither man would have been

65. The railway rivalries are discussed in some detail in Arthur W. Thompson, "The Railroad Background of the Florida Senatorial Election of 1851," *Florida Historical Quarterly*, XXXI (January, 1953), 181-195.
66. Florida *Senate Journal* (1850-1851), pp. 278-279.

their choice had they the power to select a Senator, but Mallory was the best they could do under the circumstances. Though leading Democrats realized that Mallory's views on sectional controversies were much the same as Yulee's, Whigs insisted that his views were unknown. As the *Sentinel* put it, the Whigs had "bought a pig in a poke."[67] Nonetheless, their object—to be rid of Yulee—was accomplished.

67. February 4, 1851.

4. DECAY AND DECLINE

The results of the election of 1850 in Florida seemed to show that Floridians were not yet ready to support the cause of secession or disunion. Yet at the same time Cabell's reduced majority and the loss of the legislature to the Democrats suggest that the confidence of the people in the Whig party had been shaken. Since there were no vital local issues in this election, this loss of confidence probably centered in the ability, or the lack of it, of the Whigs to protect the vital interests of the South. Throughout Florida, as throughout the rest of the South, the year 1851 saw the formation of Southern Rights associations and Constitutional Union clubs. Both movements aimed at rallying Southerners of both parties to their banners and both had a measure of success, but over the long run the Southern Rights groups won out. Generally the leadership of the latter was in the hands of radical Democrats, while the Union movement was in the hands of Whigs.

Neither Southern nor Northern extremists were willing to accept the Compromise, and as the months went on, the extremes grew in influence and numbers at the expense of the moderate middle ground. In 1851, however, the middle-of-the-road groups seemed to have triumphed. Daniel Webster noted with sarcasm that all politicians were now saying "they always meant to stand by the Union to the last."[1] The Congressional short session of 1850-1851 was held in an atmosphere of great good feeling and cordiality and the phrase "the finality of the Compromise" was on all lips. Among the Democrats moderates were for a time strengthened, and talk of secession gave way to acceptance of the Compromise and an emphasis on Southern "rights."[2]

In Florida pro-Union public meetings were held, usually by Whigs, though one was sponsored in Key West by Democrats. The *Sentinel* expressed Whig approval of the Union movement and took favorable notice of attempts to organize a Union party, particularly in Georgia. It declared that "whenever a Union party shall be

---

1. Allan Nevins, *Ordeal of the Union* (2 vols., New York, 1947), I, 346.
2. Nevins, I, 348-349; Avery O. Craven, *The Growth of Southern Nationalism, 1848-1861* (Baton Rouge, La., 1953), p. 121.

organized on broad, generous, liberal, constitutional ground, we propose to be with it."[3] Conservative Union meetings were soon noted in the North as well, and in New York businessmen and merchants gave much time and money to the movement. These were aimed at weakening the free-soil forces in both parties.

Promoters of the Union party in the South were using an appeal which the sectionalists had used in the 1840's. They urged the uniting of all Southerners into one party, but they would have this party cooperate with Northern conservatives to control the Union and stifle extremists. Richard K. Call urged such action upon Floridians. He pointed out that if all conservatives submerged their "party strife," extremists would not be able to play them off against each other. If a national Union party could not be formed on such grounds, then, he urged, a Southern Union party should be formed not for sectional purposes but to hold the balance between the opposing political parties of the North.[4]

Representative Cabell became an advocate of a Union party early in 1852, as he became increasingly fearful of the disruption of the Whig party. In the North the Clay-Webster Whigs were sharply dividing from the free-soil Whigs, and the latter were growing in influence. Southerners who had endorsed the Compromise had almost universally warned that the fugitive slave law provision must be honored by the North. Yet as the fifties grew on, free-soil Whigs everywhere were rejecting that law and attempting to nullify it through the action of local governments.[5]

Cabell spoke on the subject of parties in the House of Representatives on February 3, 1852, charging that the Northern Whig party had run wild on the slavery question. Yet he went on to urge that the Union party movements of the South should ally themselves with the Whig party because the Whig free-soilers were going over to the Democrats and Southern Whigs and Northern Union Whigs were the only dependable allies of the Unionists. Though a Whig, he pointed out that he had given all aid in his power to the Union associations in the South and had tried to induce the Whigs of Florida to unite themselves with a Constitutional Union party. He

3. Tallahassee *Florida Sentinel,* February 18, 1851.
4. R. K. Call to Joseph Clisby, November 29, 1851, *ibid.,* December 2, 1851.
5. Nevins, I, 350-353.

strongly urged the nomination of Millard Fillmore as the Whig presidential candidate and warned that a different nominee might render impossible the survival of the Whig party in the South. When asked if he would support Winfield Scott, he answered: "unhesitatingly, NO. I will not support him, but will do all in my power to defeat the election of any man who, in such times as these, withholds his opinions from the public," and he added, " . . . I think I express the sentiment of the Southern Whig Party."[6] Cabell was in close association with Robert Toombs and Alexander H. Stephens of Georgia in supporting the Union movement and in opposing Scott.

In the two years after 1850, two things that stand out are the fluidity that came to national political lines and the damage that was done to political parties. Not only were there rifts between Northern and Southern wings of the parties, but there were divisions within each of those wings. The Whig party which had done the most to promote the Compromise was the worst sufferer from its strains and stresses. Its Northern wing was torn apart when the free-soil forces bitterly assailed the Clay-Webster Compromise Whigs. Its Southern organizations in several instances had lost their solidarity in the short-lived Union movements which had sought to bring together Southern Democrats and Whigs in one organization. In Florida the Union party movement had never been as strong as, for instance, it had been in Alabama or Georgia, and old party lines seemed stronger. Yet as the free-soil elements came to dominate Northern Whiggery, the Florida Whigs increasingly found themselves at odds with the national Whigs, and the Florida leaders became more nervously defensive about their predicament.

The Democrats, better organized and older as a party, suffered less than the Whigs, and their Southern organizations with the help of big city machines determined to keep their national party "right" on slavery. The Florida Democrats in 1852 began to modify their program, soft-pedaling the disunionists. Democratic papers portrayed their party as the great party of the South which had never thought of breaking up the Union, while the Democratic state convention in April, 1852, adopted an inoffensive platform deprecating the "mischievous and unwise" agitation of the slavery question. The Whig *Sentinel* observed that the platform planks "mean

6. *Congressional Globe,* 32 Congress, 1 Session, pp. 451-456.

whatever interpretation may be put upon them, and do credit to the political tact of the gentlemen who drew them."[7]

For governor the Democrats chose James E. Broome, after nine ballots. A Leon County planter, Broome had come from South Carolina in 1837 and had been a vigorous opponent of the Compromise of 1850. The *Florida Whig* described him as "a Secessionist in the abstract and the concrete, of the strictest sect of the South Carolina separationists." As a concession to the moderates, Augustus E. Maxwell was nominated to oppose Cabell in the Congressional race. Maxwell had been a defender of the Compromise and was unanimously chosen on the first ballot. Even the *Whig* conceded that he was "generally popular."[8]

Gagging at the attempt of Democratic papers to paint their party as the defender of the Compromise and to whitewash Broome's extremism, the editor of the *Sentinel* incredulously cried: "Do they imagine . . . that they can cause the people to forget their course but a short time ago, when some of them declared that the Compromise 'tore the Constitution to tatters,' and that they 'would rather see the Union dissolved than the adoption of Compromise Measures?' "[9]

The Whig campaign opened with spirited county meetings designed to rally the people behind the Compromise as a final settlement of sectional issues. The first meeting, in Gadsden County, issued a call for a state-wide Whig convention, endorsed the Compromise and Fillmore, and named delegates to the proposed state convention. Ward was suggested for the governorship and Cabell for Congress. Though many Whigs were cool to the idea of a convention, it gradually gained support.[10]

Meanwhile reports came from Washington of a caucus of the Whig members of Congress to call a national convention. Southerners had tried to have the caucus commit the convention in advance to support the finality of the Compromise, but they had been overruled. A number of Southern Whigs thereupon walked out and joined in publishing an "Address of Southern Whigs to Whigs of the United States." In it they declared that they had wished to induce the Whig party to assume national grounds by

7. April 27, 1852.
8. Quoted in Tallahassee *Florida Sentinel,* May 11, 1852; see also June 22, 1852.
9. *Ibid.,* June 8, 1852.   10. *Ibid.,* May 4, 1852.

endorsing the Compromise and terminating agitation on the slavery question. They predicted the defeat of the party if such action were not taken.[11] The schism in the national party was daily growing.

Whig county meetings in Florida continued to be held in Jackson, Santa Rosa, Jefferson, Marion, Columbia, and Duval counties. In Duval resolutions were adopted endorsing tariff and internal improvement views and smacking of "native Americanism." Two speakers, J. P. Sanderson and James W. Bryant, voiced their willingness to desert the Whigs if free-soil forces controlled the national convention. Sanderson was later a presidential-elector candidate, and Bryant was a delegate to the national convention. The place and time for the state convention were finally set by the Middle Florida district meeting which designated July 14 at Tallahassee.[12]

On the eve of the Whig National Convention, which opened at Baltimore on June 16, Cabell rose again in the House of Representatives to hurl a warning at the Northern wing of his party. The Compromise measures, he cautioned, must be sustained and a candidate chosen who would uphold them. While he conceded that he did not intend to join the Democratic party "and adopt its principles and heresies," still he threatened that "if Northern Whigs cannot meet us here; if they are resolved to go on with the slavery agitation, and to repeal the fugitive slave law, the party ought not to be preserved." Pointedly he attacked the candidacy of Winfield Scott and pressed the claims of Fillmore to the presidency.[13]

The Whig National Convention rather rapidly and easily approved a platform accepting the Compromise as a final settlement of the questions which it embraced. Members of the extreme antislavery wing immediately charged a bargain by party managers by which a Southern platform would be given in exchange for Southern acceptance of Scott. The charge probably was not without foundation. Several Southern delegates switched to Scott, who triumphed over Fillmore and Webster on the fifty-third ballot. William A. Graham of North Carolina was then named for the vice-presidency. As it turned out, the staunchest Southern Whigs would take Scott, but they were a minority.[14] The extreme antislavery men walked

11. *Ibid.*   12. *Ibid.*, May 18, 25, June 1, 15, 1852.
13. *Congressional Globe*, 32 Congress, 1 Session, pp. 682-685.
14. Nevins, II, 27-29; Tallahassee *Florida Sentinel*, June 29, 1852.

out and named their own presidential and vice-presidential candidates in another convention.

Florida Whig papers were generally disappointed, but decided to accept Scott. The *Pensacola Gazette* said nothing more could be asked of Scott than that he stand on the platform. The *Sentinel* countered charges that Seward was backing Scott with the news that Van Buren supported the Democratic nominee, but acknowledged that Floridians had a special reason to dislike Scott. The "reasons of a local character" which made Scott so distasteful to Floridians arose from an order which he had issued during the Indian war in 1836. Its substance was a criticism of the civilian population of Florida for showing what Scott termed panic and cowardice in the face of Indian depredations. Scott tried to remedy the situation in 1852 by stating that new information had caused him to believe that his censures had been unmerited.[15] The damage, however, had been done.

The Democratic National Convention in Baltimore had meanwhile chosen Franklin Pierce and William R. King to head their ticket and had pledged adherence to the Compromise and an end to slavery agitation. Pierce was not encumbered with any past national record and was a highly "available" candidate. Since the two-thirds rule prevailed in the Democratic convention, the South had a larger voice both in the naming of candidates and the adoption of principles than it did in the Whig convention. In a great ratification meeting in Tallahassee, Augustus Maxwell was enthusiastically applauded when he extolled Pierce as a great defender of the Compromise. The *Sentinel* reported, however, that when James E. Broome rose in the same assembly and stated his opposition to the Compromise, he received as great an ovation as had Maxwell in praising it.[16]

The Whig state convention met in July at Tallahassee and was clearly under the control of the staunchest old party leaders. Richard K. Call was chosen presiding officer, and Lewis I. Fleming and Columbus Drew were secretaries. George T. Ward explained to the convention the events that had transpired in Baltimore, and the nominees of the national convention were approved, with only

15. *Pensacola Gazette,* June 26, 1852; Tallahassee *Florida Sentinel,* July 6, 1852; Winfield Scott to Thomas Randall, June 7, 1852, in *Pensacola Gazette,* August 21, 1852.   16. June 15, 22, 1852.

the representatives of Gadsden County voting in the negative. The convention then nominated Ward for the governorship and Cabell for Congress. After the nominations, however, the convention was plunged into a tumultuous controversy when a letter arrived from Cabell declaring his intention not to support Scott under any conditions. Ward's reaction was a flat refusal to be a candidate on the same ticket with Cabell. A secret session followed at which attempts were reportedly made to strike Cabell from the ticket, but they were not successful. The convention then nominated both Ward and Cabell again, and great pressures were brought to bear upon Cabell who ultimately agreed to "acquiesce" in the nomination of Scott.[17]

After the convention adjourned, the Democratic Jacksonville *News* reported the death of the Whig party "by political suicide," and added: "The body will be embalmed and kept over ground till *November,* when it will be laid in a grave."[18] The *Floridian* taunted the Whigs, saying that surely no Democrat who had previously admired Cabell's independence could now support him for re-election. While the *Pensacola Gazette* explained away Cabell's repudiation of Scott as due to the bad influence of such men as Robert Toombs and Alexander H. Stephens of Georgia, Cabell himself simply stated that he had believed he was fighting the fight of his people and that "if I have erred at all it is from too great zeal in the advocacy of a righteous cause."[19] The career of the popular young Congressman was dying of the sickness of the Whig party.

During the campaign in the state more attention was devoted to the gubernatorial race than had hitherto been the case. This interest stemmed from the fact that Broome was considered the leader of the radical "South Carolina school" in Florida. The lines were sharply drawn between Broome and Ward, the latter an ultraconservative Unionist standing squarely on the Whig national platform. By contrast, in the Congressional race both Cabell and Maxwell were defenders of moderate measures and sectional conciliation. Ward was joined in his campaign by the incumbent governor, Thomas

17. *Pensacola Gazette,* July 24, 31, 1852; Dorothy Dodd, "The Secession Movement in Florida, 1850-1861," *Florida Historical Quarterly,* XII (July, 1933), p. 16.
18. Quoted in *Pensacola Gazette,* August 14, 1852.
19. Tallahassee *Floridian,* August 21, 1852; *Pensacola Gazette,* July 31, 1852; Tallahassee *Florida Sentinel,* September 28, 1852.

Brown, who fought Broome almost as vigorously as if he were the Whig candidate himself. The Whig press etched in sharp lines the picture of Broome as a secessionist, a radical, a destroyer of the Union.[20]

When the official returns were compiled, Broome was found to have defeated Ward by 292 votes, 4,628 to 4,336. Maxwell defeated Cabell by only 22 votes, 4,590 to 4,568. In addition, the Democrats won decisive control of both houses of the General Assembly. "The Whigs of little Florida," wrote the *Sentinel*, "have gone down with the national flag at their masthead, in a gallant struggle, under the most unfavorable circumstances, to uphold the integrity and nationality of the Whig party."[21]

The presidential election followed the next month, and Pierce and King swept all before them. Interest in Florida had dropped considerably between the two elections, however, and 1,996 fewer votes were cast in November than in October. The Whig presidential electors carried only Nassau, Walton, and Holmes counties.[22] The results of this election were a bitter vindication of the fears and futile efforts of Cabell. He, more than any other Whig leader in Florida, realized that the party schism was real, was serious, and was virtually impossible to compromise. It was this realization which motivated his fruitless search for new alignments and which explains his interest in the Union party movement.

In contrast to the Whigs, the Democrats had made great efforts during the winter of 1851-1852 to reorganize and reunite their party. Under the pressure of popular opinion the national party had accepted the "finality of the Compromise," and the Florida branch of the organization had made a quick about-face to show a moderate, more conciliatory attitude. This fact, taken in conjunction with the internal dissension of the Whigs, goes far to explain the trend to the Democrats in Florida. The fact, too, that Democratic state nominees in 1852 were taken from both moderate and extreme factions possibly attracted a wider range of voters. The rapid growth of the state and the patterns of immigration into it also had some influence. Between 1850 and 1860 the number of South-Carolina-born inhabitants in Florida almost doubled, and the number of Georgians increased by about 50 per cent. The largest

20. Tallahassee *Florida Sentinel*, September 28, 1852.
21. *Ibid.*, October 19, November 23, 1852. 22. *Ibid.*, December 7, 1852.

number of nonnative Floridians were from Georgia and South Carolina, in that order, and together they constituted about one-third of the total population by 1860. One would expect that much of the new population of the forties and fifties went to the frontier regions of East and South Florida, but some of it must have gone to the old Middle Florida regions and influenced to some degree the shift of the old Whig counties into the Democratic column.

The most important change in the election map of 1852 was the loss of both Gadsden and Leon counties by Cabell and Ward. Traditionally Whig counties, their defection put the richest part of Florida's black-belt into the hands of the Democrats. Leon and Gadsden, with traditionally Democratic Jefferson County, were the top three counties from the standpoint of slave population, cash value of farms, bales of cotton produced, and sources of revenue for the state government. They were not the largest counties from the standpoint of white population, though Gadsden was first, Leon was third, and Jefferson was sixth.[23]

Cabell lost three counties in East Florida—Alachua, Marion, and St. Johns—which he had carried in 1850. He had carried Marion in 1848 and had tied it in 1846. Surprisingly, however, he added three East Florida counties—Nassau, Columbia, and Orange—which he had not carried in 1850. None of these counties had a large slave population, except Nassau where it was on the decrease. His opposition to Scott may have been influential in these acquisitions, since Scott was particularly unpopular in the East, where most of the Indian war had been fought. On the other hand, considering the narrowness of his defeat, it may well be that the decisive factor in the Congressional race was Cabell's "acquiescence" in Scott's nomination.

The decisive Democratic sweep in 1852 left the Florida Whigs confused and dispirited. Gradually the old leaders seemed to be dropping away, and young men were coming to be attracted to the Democrats. In 1852 both Daniel Webster and Henry Clay died, and with them died the most important conservative influences among the Northern Whigs. In Florida Cabell left the political scene to become president of the Pensacola and Georgia Railroad, and in 1859 he moved to Missouri where he spent the remainder

23. *Seventh Census of the United States: 1850* (Washington, 1853), pp. 400-408.

of his life. Only the three larger Whig papers still survived, the *Florida Sentinel,* the *Florida Republican,* and the *Pensacola Gazette.* Throughout 1853 there was little to arouse political interest among Whigs, and the columns of their press were mostly occupied with business news and reports of Southern commercial conventions.

By 1854, however, sectional issues had been newly inflamed by the Kansas-Nebraska Bill. This bill in large measure grew out of the desire of business interests of the old Northwest, among whom Stephen A. Douglas was important, to have a transcontinental railroad built on a Northern route. The bill, largely managed by Douglas, was enacted to organize territorial government in the areas through which such a railroad would run. To avoid fanning the slavery issue into flame again, and to get Southern support for the bill, Douglas was willing to leave the question of slavery to be settled by the people in the area being organized. Though the implication of this was that the Missouri Compromise of 1820 was invalidated, a Southern Whig move to amend the bill so as explicitly to repeal the Missouri Compromise was successful. Defenders of the Kansas-Nebraska Act tried to argue that the 1850 Compromise had already repealed the Missouri Compromise, but to no avail. Northern opinion was shocked at the invalidation of what had come to be viewed as a solemn compact, a hallowed tradition, and a storm of controversy and indignation was let loose in the nation.[24]

Florida Democrats, remembering that in 1850 their failure to write a state platform was attacked by the Whigs as reflecting their confusion about sectional issues, began to raise objections in 1854 to holding a state convention. The *Ancient City* declared that a convention would be inexpedient, and the *Republican* reported that some Democrats were fearful that the convention might drop incumbent Representative Maxwell as the 1846 convention had dropped Brockenbrough. Nevertheless, a convention was scheduled for Madison in July.[25]

Meanwhile, a Whig meeting in St. Johns County suggested a party convention at Lake City, then called "Alligator," and other counties endorsed the idea. The *Sentinel* was cool toward a state convention, but the *Republican* urged one so that united support

24. Nevins, II, 95-96, 109; Wilfred C. Binkley, *American Political Parties* (New York, 1947), pp. 109-191.
25. Jacksonville *Florida Republican,* June 29, 1854.

for the candidates might be obtained. The latter paper took note of the Kansas-Nebraska Act and reported that it had serious objections to the measure, but that it approved of the repeal of the Missouri Compromise.[26]

At Madison the Democrats approved the Kansas-Nebraska Bill as "a measure conceived in a spirit of justice to all the States" and renominated Maxwell for Congress.[27] The Whigs dropped the idea of a state convention, after St. Johns and Duval County meetings had endorsed Thomas Brown for Congress and had agreed to dispensing with the state meeting. Brown had earlier been put forward by Leon and Gadsden counties. The local issues in this race for Congress were either personal or of little consequence. Whigs emphasized the attraction of Brown to "the solitary backwoodsmen and pioneers," called for a tariff on Canadian lumber, and defended the right of the people to cut light wood on the public land. Democrats urged a fusion of Whigs and Democrats in the light of what was happening to the national Whig party, but Whigs insisted that there was no reason why party lines should not be maintained in local elections.[28]

Brown swept aside petty issues and conducted his campaign largely on the Kansas-Nebraska issue. He charged that Democrats who had introduced the measure had reopened the slavery controversy, thus violating their pledge to the "finality" of the Compromise of 1850. Had he been in Congress, he affirmed, he would have opposed consideration of the measure. He trimmed a bit, however, in admitting that had he failed in blocking its consideration he would have voted for it. His support would have been given because it repealed the Missouri Compromise, which was in his view merely a forerunner of the Wilmot Proviso. This curious attitude was perhaps a concession to growing Southern hostility toward measures restrictive of slavery. Some Whigs felt that Brown's record as governor might be interpreted as lacking concern for Southern rights, and the attempt was made in this campaign to give him a more pronounced pro-Southern coloration.[29]

The Whig cause could not be saved, however. Except in Gadsden

26. *Ibid.,* July 13, 27, 30, August 3, 1854.   27. *Ibid.,* August 3, 1854.
28. *Ibid.,* August 10, 17, 24, September 7, 1854.
29. *Ibid.,* September 28, 1854; Tallahassee *Florida Sentinel,* August 29, 1854.

County, the Middle Florida planters who left the party in 1852 did not come back, and enough voters deserted the Whigs in Wakulla and the western stronghold of Escambia to lose those counties for them. In the East, of the six counties which Cabell had carried in 1852, Brown lost Columbia, Putnam, and Levy, and added only Hamilton, where there had been a tie vote in 1852. About 1,000 more votes were cast in 1854 than in 1852, and one might assume that the new voters were all Democrats. Whereas Cabell had lost in 1852 by 22 votes, Brown lost by 1,074. Maxwell was victorious, 5,638 to 4,564.[30]

After the Congressional election of 1854 the Whig party never again functioned on a state-wide basis in Florida. This election did not mark the end of the two-party system in the state, however, even though it did emphasize the fact of Democratic dominance in Florida politics. Less than two months after this election Whig papers began to take notice of the "Know Nothing" movement, and in 1855 the larger portion of old Whig leaders identified themselves with the movement, which called itself the American party. Formal organization of the party came at a state convention in Tallahassee in November, 1855. Presiding over it was Thomas Brown, and old-line Whigs clearly dominated the gathering. Richard K. Call played a prominent role in the American National Convention in 1856, where he turned down moves to nominate him for the vice-presidency and successfully nominated for that office Andrew J. Donelson.[31] Millard Fillmore was the presidential candidate. As in the Whig convention of 1852, radical antislavery men split off from the American convention. In 1856, however, they became Republicans.

In the 1855 local elections the Americans, and candidates still calling themselves Whigs, made encouraging headway in areas where the Whigs had been traditionally strong. Though the main strength of the American party lay among the old Whigs, some Whigs had become Democrats, while some Democrats had become Americans. Notable examples of these two trends were George W. Call, Jr., and William W. McCall. Call, an ex-Whig, was a Democratic presidential elector in 1856, while McCall, an ex-Democrat, was an American presidential elector. The American state slate was

30. Tallahassee *Florida Sentinel*, November 23, 1852, November 7, 1854.
31. *Ibid.*, November 28, 1854, September 11, December 11, 1855; Jacksonville *Florida Republican*, March 6, 1856.

David S. Walker for governor and James M. Baker for Congress-man. The Democrats named Madison S. Perry for the governorship and George S. Hawkins for Congress. Perry, like his predecessor, Broome, was of the radical wing of the party, as was also Hawkins, a former New York lawyer.[32]

The Democrats decisively won all of the state-wide races, Ameri-can strength being for the most part in old Whig regions. In the General Assembly the Democrats retained control, 29 to 16 in the House and 13 to 7 in the Senate. There had been virtually no change in the relative strength of the Democrats and their opponents in the legislature since 1852. This control had enabled the Demo-crats to return Yulee to the Senate in 1855 in place of Morton. The Democratic triumph of 1856 and the split in the national American party were correctly viewed by men on both sides as the death blow to the American party in Florida.[33]

In 1858 there was no organized political opposition to the Demo-crats, though John Westcott, with the support of Governor Perry, tried to unseat Representative Hawkins, who was supported by Yulee. Westcott ran as an "Independent Democrat," but he made a poor showing and was defeated. The major point of contention among Democrats in this race was rivalry over railroad interests.[34] Not until 1860 did the old Whigs again bestir themselves to a last effort against the Democrats, this time in the guise of the Constitu-tional Union party. In the spring and summer of 1860 county meetings were held all over the state, and a state convention at Quincy named delegates to a national convention which nominated John Bell of Tennessee for president and Edward Everett of Massa-chusetts for vice-president. The state convention chose for the gov-ernorship Edward Hopkins, an ex-Whig, and for Congress Benjamin F. Allen, an ex-Whig and editor of the *Florida Sentinel*.[35]

Union or secession were the only issues of this election, and on

32. Jacksonville *Florida Republican*, October 4, 11, 18, 1855, July 16, 1856; Tallahassee *Floridian*, June 28, 1856; Dodd, "Secession Movement," p. 22.

33. Tallahassee *Floridian*, November 29, 1856; Jacksonville *Florida Republican*, November 26, 1856.

34. Jacksonville *Florida News*, August 28, 1858, March 17, 1859. See also Thompson, "Political Nativism in Florida, 1848-1860," *Journal of South-ern History*, XV (February, 1949), 61.

35. Fernandina *East Floridian*, May 17, July 19, 1860.

their demand for secession if Lincoln should be elected, the Democrats carried all before them. Again the Constitutional Union Party made a good showing where the Whigs and the Americans had been strong.[36] The Americans and the Unionists can both be classified as conservative, antisecession parties which tried to regroup dissident elements into an opposition party to replace the defunct Whig organization. The leaders of all these parties were the same men. After their defeat in 1860, a few of the most ardent of these conservatives turned their efforts toward slowing the tide toward secession. Richard K. Call, George T. Ward, and Columbus Drew were notable in this unsuccessful effort.

For most of these older men, their day was done. Yet some of the younger Whigs lived on and played political roles during the Civil War and afterward. Probably most notable of them was Richard Call's nephew Wilkinson Call. A staunch Whig, a defender of the Americans and the Constitutional Unionists, young Call lived on to become a United States Senator, serving from 1879 to 1897 as a liberal Democrat. Other Whigs who played prominent parts in postwar politics included David S. Walker, governor 1866-1868; Ossian B. Hart, Republican governor 1873-1874; George F. Drew, Democratic governor 1877-1881; John L. Crawford, Democratic secretary of state 1881-1889; Benjamin F. Allen, secretary of state 1863-1868; Robert H. Gamble, comptroller 1868-1873; Columbus Drew, Democratic comptroller 1877-1881; and Jesse J. Finley, intermittently Democratic member of the United States House of Representatives between 1876 and 1882, and briefly United States Senator in 1887.

36. Tallahassee *Floridian,* November 17, 1860.

5. WHO WERE THE FLORIDA WHIGS?

Studies of the Whig party in the South generally have assumed a close correlation between the Whig strongholds and the heavy slaveholding and cotton-producing areas. To a considerable extent that general pattern was true in Florida. Though it is true, as it was throughout the South, that planters and great slaveholders and men of wealth were to be found in both parties, the fact that Whig strength centered in the rich plantation counties should not be minimized. In Florida, as elsewhere, the planters were generally the leaders in public affairs and were in the minority in the population. Clearly neither party could have won success had it depended solely upon that class for support. Yet it is such an intangible thing as the influence of this class, which cannot be statistically measured, which must be looked to for one of the keys to political alignment. In certain areas of Florida the "big" men were Whigs, and they exerted an important political influence upon the small farmers, professional men, overseers, merchants, shippers, and craftsmen. There was a definite correlation, as will be shown, between property ownership and political affiliation. Whigs in Florida tended to be men of greater property holdings than were Democrats.

In the eleven counties which were strongholds of Whiggery in Florida, the proportions of slave to white populations varied considerably, ranging from about one slave for every ten whites in Holmes County to eight slaves for every three whites in Leon County. Yet these were extremes, for in five of those eleven counties (Jackson, Gadsden, Madison, Nassau, Duval) the slave-white populations were about equal in number. In the remaining four the discrepancy was not great, the slave-white ratio being in Wakulla one to one and one-half, in Escambia one to two, in Santa Rosa one to two and one-half, and in Walton one to four. By contrast, in the twelve counties which were Democratic strongholds, only one (Jefferson) had more slaves than whites. The ratio there was about two slaves to one white. In none of the other Democratic strongholds did the slave population approach equality with the whites in numbers. St. Johns County, with 1,417 whites to 993 slaves, came closest to balancing. Dade County was most disproportionate, having 147 whites to 11 slaves. Of the five counties which cannot be counted strong-holds of either party the slave-white ratio in two was one to three, in two others one to two, and in the fifth it was about even. The total slave population of the eleven Whig counties was 25,883 as compared with 13,639 in the twelve Democratic counties. The five uncommitted counties numbered their slave total at 3,778.[1]

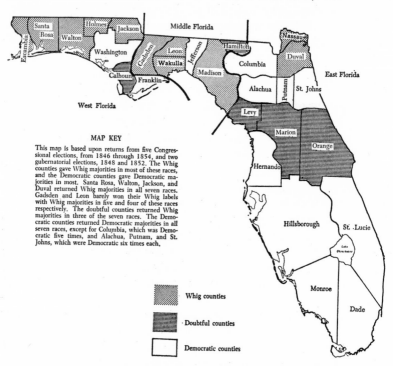

MAP KEY

This map is based upon returns from five Congres-sional elections, from 1846 through 1854, and two gubernatorial elections, 1848 and 1852. The Whig counties gave Whig majorities in most of these races, and the Democratic counties gave Democratic ma-jorities in most. Santa Rosa, Walton, Jackson, and Duval returned Whig majorities in all seven races. Gadsden and Leon barely won their Whig labels with Whig majorities in five and four of these races respectively. The doubtful counties returned Whig majorities in three of the seven races. The Demo-cratic counties returned Democratic majorities in all seven races, except for Columbia, which was Demo-cratic five times, and Alachua, Putnam, and St. Johns, which were Democratic six times each.

Whig counties

Doubtful counties

Democratic counties

The total valuation placed on the farm land of these eleven Whig counties was $4,187,391, as contrasted with $1,416,113 for ten Democratic counties. (Two of the Democratic counties made no returns on farm land values.) It is also interesting that the value of land in one Whig stronghold, Leon County, was $1,751,959, or slightly more than one-third the value of land in all eleven Whig counties, and more than the value of all the ten Democratic counties reporting. While all the Whig counties were not big cotton pro-

1. *Seventh Census of the United States: 1850* (Washington, 1853), pp. 400-401, 407.

ducers, all the big cotton-producing counties were Whig strongholds except one, Jefferson County. More Democratic counties than Whig counties were tobacco-growing areas, but the greatest volume of tobacco was raised in six Whig counties with one, Gadsden, producing in 1850 more tobacco than all the rest of the state. One of the eastern Whig strongholds, Nassau County, was the state's rice-growing center, producing 404,305 pounds of rice in 1850, four times as much as its nearest rival, Columbia County.

Four of the top five counties in the state, so far as value of farm land, number of bales of cotton produced, number of slaves, and size of white population are concerned, were Whig counties. They were Leon, Gadsden, Madison, and Jackson counties. These might be termed "typical" Whig counties in that the dominant interests in them most closely resemble the conventional idea of the interests that composed the Southern Whig party. While these plantation Whig counties of Middle Florida were generally the backbone of Whig strength, there were also Whig strongholds that were commercial centers rather than rich agricultural areas. Duval County in the East and Escambia County in the West fit into this category. Duval was the home of the port of Jacksonville, which in the 1850's was the center of an extensive lumber industry. It was also the port through which the agricultural produce of all East Florida drained by the St. Johns River was shipped out to the world. Escambia County was the home of the port of Pensacola, where lumbering was important, but probably the exporting of cotton from southern Alabama was of more importance. The Alabama regions contiguous to Escambia were heavily Whig, as was the territory drained by the rivers emptying into Pensacola Bay. The little East Florida county of Nassau, which boasted the largest rice production, also was noted for its commercial activities, centering in Fernandina, which sat at the mouth of the St. Mary's River, the river draining southern Georgia and extreme northern Florida.

The strongholds of the Democratic party in Florida were for the most part the thinly populated poorer counties which usually had more whites than slaves. The staunchest Democratic counties were the sparsely settled South Florida counties of Hernando, Hillsborough, St. Lucie, Monroe, and Dade, the two small West Florida counties, Washington and Franklin, and the rich Middle Florida county of Jefferson. Very close behind these counties in their devotion to Democratic candidates were the North Florida counties of Columbia, Alachua, Putnam, and St. Johns. The counties which showed no consistent loyalty to the candidates of either party were Levy, Marion, and Orange in East Florida, Hamilton in Middle Florida, and Calhoun in West Florida.

In the columns of both parties were counties which defy the generalizations which have been laid down. Jefferson County, among the Democratic strongholds, is one such. It ranked third in value of farm lands, second in bales of cotton produced, and second in number of slaves. About 65 per cent of the population was slave in 1850. Despite these facts, and the fact that it was surrounded by Whig counties, it never returned a Whig majority in any state-wide race and never elected a Whig to the state legislature. There is no clearly apparent explanation for the position of Jefferson County. The only evidence contributing to an explanation which this writer has found is a survey of twenty-six important plantations in the county which showed that ten of them were settled by South Carolinians. This, compared to the fact that five were settled by Georgians, four each by Virginians and North Carolinians, and one each by natives of New York, Kentucky, and Tennessee, would seem to indicate that the South Carolina and Georgia planters were more influential in the county than any other group. Georgians and South Carolinians were more often than not Democrats, as we shall later statistically show, and this is borne out in this specific case in reference to the particular individuals examined by this survey.[2] In addition the manuscript census returns show 1,178 of Jefferson County's 2,775 whites were born in Georgia and South Carolina, a considerably higher proportion than for the state as a whole.

Whig counties which do not fit the conventional pattern are the West Florida group, Santa Rosa, Walton, and Holmes. All were staunchly Whig, though they were poor, thinly populated counties producing practically no cotton or tobacco and having few slaves. Explanatory factors may be derived from the facts that all bordered on heavy Whig areas in Alabama, and that Holmes was formed from Jackson, which was the banner Whig county of the state. Santa Rosa and Walton were both astride the water routes from the southern Alabama cotton fields to Pensacola's docks.

2. "Jefferson County Plantations," compiled by the Federal Writers Project, W. P. A. (typescript), in P. K. Yonge Library of Florida History.

Two unusual counties in West Florida bear further examination. Calhoun and Franklin, located at the mouth of the Apalachicola River, were bitter rivals for the business of that great stream. Franklin, in which the city of Apalachicola was located, was a Democratic stronghold. By the measure of Duval and Escambia, which were commercial centers, it should have been Whig, for much of its income was derived from shipping the cotton which came down the Apalachicola and its tributaries from Georgia and Alabama. However, unlike the situation in both Duval and Escambia, the rivers which joined to form the Apalachicola River drained areas in Georgia and Alabama which were heavily populated, long settled, and largely Democratic in politics. Calhoun County boasted of St. Joseph as its leading city. Its developers, who were in large measure bank men, planters, and land speculators who were Whigs, sought by various railroad and canal schemes to divert the lucrative traffic which Apalachicola enjoyed. The efforts of this group were well known, thanks to the *Apalachicola Gazette*. These facts, taken together, help to explain why Franklin was Democratic and why Calhoun alternated.

Until 1850 the main appeal of the Whig party was to the propertied and commercial interests, their dependent classes, and those under their influence. These men were attracted by the down-to-earth, materialistic goals of the party—banks, benefits and protections for business interests, stimulation of internal improvements, relatively sound financial policies, and the promotion of education —and they were annoyed by the Democrats' more abstract goals— political democracy, equality of opportunity, and restriction of corporate privilege. By 1850, however, the material goals of the Whigs had become subordinated to that of the preservation of the Union, and in Florida this brand of Whig nationalism seems temporarily to have attracted agrarian interests, large and small, of such strong Northeast Florida Democratic counties as Columbia, St. Johns, Putnam, and Alachua. When the national Whigs split on this very issue, many of these interests returned to their old loyalties, and many Florida Whigs went with them, as local Democrats seemed to lose their concern for the abstract principles they had promoted in the 1830's and 1840's and as the Democratic party remained the one national political organization in the country.

Judging from analyses of county voting records, then, the people who were the backbone of Whig voting strength in Florida were the

67

large-scale cotton and tobacco planters of Middle and West Florida, with their dependent classes and the small farmers within their influence; the cotton and rice planters, lumber men, and shippers of East Florida; the commercial and lumber interests of extreme West Florida; and the covetous merchants and speculators of St. Joseph, eyeing the lucrative trade of Apalachicola.

An analysis of a different sort seems to confirm these generalizations in large measure. The backgrounds of the individual citizens who took part in Florida politics fall into a general pattern which does not do violence to these generalizations. For the purposes of this second analysis, the record of all state legislators from 1845 through 1854, of all candidates for governor, representative, and register of lands, and of all United States Senators between 1845 and 1854, were sought out. The attempt was to find the age, the occupation, the place of birth, the number of slaves, and the value of the real estate of each of these political figures. In most instances the information was found.[3]

In regard to the state legislators, it was theoretically possible for 311 men to have held seats in the General Assembly between 1845 and 1854. Because of the fact that many men served several times, as closely as this writer can compute, 237 men actually served in the General Assembly during that time. Of that number the party affiliations of 4 could not be ascertained, and census enumerations of 37 could not be found. The analysis of legislators, therefore, is based on the remaining 196—82 Whigs and 114 Democrats—who could be identified in the Census of 1850, that is, about 82 per cent of the men who actually sat in the Assembly.

So far as slaveholding is concerned, the difference between Whig legislators and Democratic legislators was not marked. Whigs, with an average of 18.8 slaves and a median of 11 slaves, tended to own slightly more than did Democrats, who averaged 14.2 slaves and had a median figure of 7 slaves. Twenty-six per cent of the Democrats reported no slaves, while only 12 per cent of the Whigs reported none.

3. Microfilm copies of the original white and slave schedules of the Seventh Census of the United States, in Yonge Library of Florida History. The term "median" used frequently in the paragraphs that follow differs from "average" in that a median designates a point so chosen in a series of property or slaveholding figures, listed in order from lowest to highest, that half of the figures are above it and half are below it.

There is a far more marked difference between Democrats and Whigs in the matter of real-estate ownership than in slaveholding. Though the average property holdings were about the same, $3,462.50 for Democrats as opposed to $3,493.29 for Whigs, the median figure reflects a greater difference. The median value of property held by Whigs was $1,850, while the Democrats' median was only $800. Thirty-seven per cent of the Democrats reported no real estate, while only 29 per cent of the Whigs reported none.

There is little difference between Whig and Democratic legislators in occupations except that more Whigs than Democrats were in the farmer class: about 42 per cent of the Whigs and about 39 per cent of the Democrats. Forty-one per cent of both Whigs and Democrats were in the business and professional classes, with the Whigs leading in lawyers, about 20 per cent to the Democrats' 17 per cent. Seven per cent of the Democrats told census enumerators they were planters, while 6 per cent of the Whigs classed themselves as such. The differentiation between farmers and planters was not clearly made, however, since many who called themselves farmers possessed slaves and property enough to be thought of as planters, while some who called themselves planters reported so few slaves and so little property that they must have been flattering themselves.

There is a more marked difference between Whigs and Democrats in regard to place of birth. Only about 6 per cent of the Whigs and 9 per cent of the Democrats were born in Florida. More Whigs, almost 28 per cent, came from North Carolina than any other single state, while the largest number of Democrats, almost 36 per cent, came from Georgia. The percentage of Democrats from states of the lower South (Florida, Georgia, South Carolina, Alabama, Mississippi) was 64.2, while only 19.9 per cent came from the upper South (Kentucky, Tennessee, Virginia, Maryland, North Carolina). With Whigs the reverse was true. Forty-one per cent of the Whigs came from the upper South, while 37.3 per cent were from the lower South. Eighteen per cent of the Whig legislators were from abroad or from Northern states. Only 13.4 per cent of the Democrats were from abroad or from the North. The average age of Democrats was almost 39 years, that of Whigs almost 42.

Whig legislators, then, tended to own a few more slaves and considerably more land than did their Democratic colleagues. Whigs tended to be slightly older than Democrats, and they were more often

69

from the North or from the upper South than were Democrats. It is probably not unusual that there was so little difference between Democrats and Whigs where occupations were concerned. The men of affairs of both parties are those who might logically be expected to take part in politics, and the breakdown in the occupational category for members of the legislature may not reflect the breakdown among Democratic and Whig voters. In this entire group of legislators, only five Democrats and five Whigs were what might be termed "working men."

Moving up the ladder to the higher political offices of state-wide importance, there were sixteen persons who were candidates, successful and unsuccessful, for the offices of governor, representative, or register of public lands between 1845 and 1854. Four served as United States Senators in the same era and one of these four, who was a candidate for representative, is included in the other sixteen so that a total of nineteen persons, seven Whigs and twelve Democrats, was under scrutiny at the higher levels of state political leadership. The average age of the Whigs was almost 48 and that of the Democrats was 44 years.

Slaveholding information was available on all of the top officials except two Democrats. The average number of slaves held by Whigs was 72 and by Democrats, 63; however, two of the ten Democrats owned no slaves and only one, William Bailey, owned more than 100. Bailey's holding of 389 Negroes was 145 more than the total owned by all the other Democrats. All of the seven Whigs were slaveholders, and three of them—E. C. Cabell, G. T. Ward, and R. K. Call—each owned 100 or more slaves. The low man was D. S. Walker, with 4 slaves, while R. K. Call was high with 143. The median for Whigs was 84, for Democrats, 18.5. Information on the holding of real property was available for six of the seven Whigs and nine of the twelve Democrats. The average value of Whig property was $25,617, while the Democrats' average was $11,278; however, five of the nine Democrats reported no real property at all, and Bailey, with property valued at $81,000, possessed almost four times as much as the remaining three property-owning Democrats. All of the Whigs reported real property, with the smallest amount being $3,000 worth reported by Walker and the largest amount being Call's $75,000 worth. The Whig median was $21,100, while technically the Democrats' median was zero.

Thus at the highest levels of leadership, where party politics and programs were shaped, the slaveholding and real-property differences between Whigs and Democrats were far sharper than at lower levels. This may be even more significant when considered in light of the fact that these men appeared before the electorate of the entire state in races which were more impersonal than the local legislative contests. In the latter, personalities and local influences could count for more than party records and principles.

Considering the fortunes of the two parties in Florida and the character of their leadership as revealed by the census returns, it may be possible to form a generalization. If we may judge by the occupancy of the governorship and the seat in the federal House of Representatives, and to a lesser extent control of the state legislature, the people of Florida turned to the men of wealth and conservatism in time of prosperity and in time of national crisis. On the other hand, they turned to the men of more moderate means and liberal or even radical views in time of financial distress, and after the leadership of the wealthy conservative group appeared inadequate in defending Southern interests in national crises.

No major political party in American history has ever been exclusively based on the support of, or on an appeal to, the interests of an "upper" or a "lower" class, though the Federalists perhaps came closest to it. The United States has been such a predominantly middle-class country that the major parties through most of our history have made their appeals to that class. This was true of the parties in ante-bellum Florida, where there were never any property qualifications for voting. Whigs and Democrats in Florida both appealed to and drew their strength from the all-pervading middle class. It is apparent, however, that the leadership of the Whig party was more predominantly drawn from the wealthy slaveholding, landowning, upper South "gentry" than was the leadership of the Democratic party.

In addition to this difference in leadership between the two parties, we should point to the doctrinal differences. The Whigs were more concerned with material progress and national unity and were less concerned with political democracy and the rights of man than were the Democrats. The Whigs also tended to represent a "status quo" outlook which established vested interests might be expected to do, while the Democrats reflected a greater sense of fluidity and change which newcomers and younger men "on the make" might be expected to do. Finally, to some extent, the party differences involved Florida's version of the tidewater versus back-country struggle. The Whigs were primarily the party of the rich, earlier settled, plantation areas of Middle Florida, while the Democrats were primarily the party of the new, frontier, small-farmer regions of East and South Florida.

An emphasis given in some scholarly circles in recent years has tended to blur the differences between American parties, and indeed this may be a needed corrective to the hasty tendency of survey histories and of the oversimplifiers to identify parties exclusively as parties of the "common man" or of the businessman or of farmers or of laborers. Such emphasis, however, renders a disservice when it leaves the impression that there was or is no difference between political parties except that one is in and one is out. Though the differences may often be differences of degree and may often appear to be slight, generally the active and influential interest groups in opposing parties have clear-cut and often sharply conflicting desires. That they hide, minimize, gloss over, and pretend that these differences do not exist is necessitated by internal compromises and by the fact that both parties seek the votes of the great middle classes and groups not concerned with their special interests—and this also makes easy the propounding of the thesis that there is no difference between parties.

That there are differences between American political parties is one generalization that it is hoped this study in small measure has helped to document.

BIBLIOGRAPHICAL NOTE

The most important sources for this study were Florida newspapers, the manuscript schedules of the United States Census of 1850, and the *Florida Historical Quarterly*. Original files of many of the newspapers are in the P. K. Yonge Library of Florida History at the University of Florida, and microfilm copies of the holdings of the Library of Congress for this period are also available there. The Yonge Library also has on film the census schedules. Two collections of the papers of Richard Keith Call, one in the Southern Historical Collection, University of North Carolina, and the other in the Florida Historical Society Library, University of Florida, were used. A few references were made to items in the Andrew Jackson Papers and the Martin Van Buren Papers in the Manuscripts Division of the Library of Congress, and to items in the State Department files at the National Archives. The files of *Niles' Weekly Register* were available in the University of Florida Library.

The footnotes will serve to provide bibliographical information about all secondary sources to which reference was made.

73